Praise for Yo...

"You'll find the 'divine woman' in your... inspiring work. Having read *You Are Divine*, I now look at all women as truly divine."

— Marcia King Gamble, bestselling author of *His Golden Heart*

"It is time for us to embrace and celebrate the femininity in us, regain our power, and redefine ourselves for the goddesses we are, in our own right. This book, to me, is a call to action, to reclaim that lost history and our true feminine powers without apology, but with pride."

—Tikiri Herath, award-winning author of the Rebel Diva series

"*You Are Divine* is a magnificently researched tribute to all women! The desire to learn, to inspire, to create, to connect, and to trust the Goddess within is the result of this must-read dedication to the Divine Feminine."

—Priscilla Connelly, LCMHC, LADC

"In her beautifully written book, Langley defines and examines those qualities we think of as feminine, encouraging us to embrace and nurture them, even as we embrace and nurture the other half of our inheritance, the 'masculine' qualities. We ... have treasured within us all the attributes of God; we need only discover and exercise them. *You Are Divine* offers help in doing that.

— Gail Radley, author of *The Night Stella Hid the Stars* and several Baha'i texts

"While reading, I found I had many shared common experiences with these women. The best part of this book are the practices at the end of each chapter, which are super helpful to dig deep, acknowledge, and honor that divine within us all."

—Mandy Nicolau Bernard, owner of Salty Dog Yoga and Surf

"At a time when traditional patriarchal ideas and mores are being questioned and renounced, Dawn Reno Langley's *You Are Divine* ... is a particularly pertinent and inspiring read. Regardless of gender or sexual identity, this book reminds the reader of the feminine energy in all of us, evoking hope for a world that has long suffered from its absence."

—Melissa B. Rooney, PhD, scientific editor and author of *The Fate of the Frog*

"*You Are Divine* ... asks [women] to explore and cherish their own goodness and strengths by providing historical and religious examples of the divine feminine from around the globe. The book spoke to me ... by taking me on a journey through the pages of history, honoring the divine females of the past, and allowing me to honor the divine."

—Dr. Shazia Rose, assistant professor at the National University of Modern Languages in Pakistan

"It is breathtaking to see [Dawn] bring her vast intelligence, creativity, and authentic self into the quest for deeper knowledge of and connection to Goddess. In following her own quest, and sharing it with us, she brings us all closer to the Divine Feminine around and within us."

— Olynda Smith, yoga teacher

"Brava to Dawn Reno Langley on *You Are Divine*—an elegant guide for nurturing the goddess spirit within. Brave, inspiring, and ever so wise."

— Char Jones, literary reviewer

"As I read, I felt women throughout the ages, both mythical and real, embrace me and whisper, 'It's true, cherished one. You really are divine.'"

—Barbara Younger, author of *Purple Mountain Majesties*

"A compelling look at how women can honor their creativity and claim their right to divinity ... This book is a go-to for all who wish to change the course of their life at any juncture and a must-read for any woman who wrestles with finding her voice and her place in the world."

— Susan Sanders, poet and coauthor of *Behind These Hills*

"In this book, Dr. Langley ... calls on all women to find the Divine Goddess that resides within them. It is an enlightening, encouraging, and illuminating book for all women of all ages."

— Nancy Christie, award-winning author of *The Gifts of Change*

YOU ARE
DIVINE

*A Search for
the Goddess in All of Us*

Dawn Reno Langley PhD

YOU ARE
DIVINE

A Search for
the Goddess in All of Us

Llewellyn Publications
Woodbury, Minnesota

FIRST EDITION
First Printing, 2022

Book design by Valerie A. King
Cover design by Shira Atakpu

Llewellyn Publications is a registered trademark of Llewellyn Worldwide Ltd.

Library of Congress Cataloging-in-Publication Data (Pending)
ISBN: 978-0-7387-6855-7

Llewellyn Worldwide Ltd. does not participate in, endorse, or have any authority or responsibility concerning private business transactions between our authors and the public.

All mail addressed to the author is forwarded but the publisher cannot, unless specifically instructed by the author, give out an address or phone number.

Any internet references contained in this work are current at publication time, but the publisher cannot guarantee that a specific location will continue to be maintained. Please refer to the publisher's website for links to authors' websites and other sources.

Llewellyn Publications
A Division of Llewellyn Worldwide Ltd.
2143 Wooddale Drive
Woodbury, MN 55125-2989
www.llewellyn.com

Printed in the United States of America

Dedication

December 16, 2017

A cold winter's day.
I light a few candles on my kitchen table where I sit at the laptop,
a copy of my notes on the right, a cup of tea to my left.
Loreena McKennitt is on Pandora,
my stained-glass lamps are lit,
and I've offered a prayer to my ancestors, my angels.
I've asked them to guide me and this book of my heart to the places
where we need to be,
to give me guidance and pave the road, help me do the best job I can:
one that will make my women ancestors and friends proud.

With a deep bow to all of the women in my life,
I begin.

Contents

Practices

Introduction: Why This Book? Why Now? Why Me?

The story behind this book starts with a woman. Not me. The story starts with Mary, mother of Jesus, wife of Joseph, the first woman I'd envisioned as divine or heavenly. In the Glendale United Methodist church where I spent my childhood, the walnut-stained, arched ceiling soared as high as a two-story building, and in alcoves by sunny windows, I caught occasional glimpses of Mary's peaceful face: the first divine female I knew.

I lived on Walnut Street in Everett, Massachusetts, just up the street from that stone church with the ten-foot-tall stained-glass windows and shiny brass pipe organ behind the pulpit. On Mondays I went to Brownies (later, Girl Scouts) in the lower meeting room; on other days, I played basketball (poorly) in the gym; sometimes I'd sneak in and sit for hours in the chapel, beneath the life-sized portrait of Jesus kneeling in the Garden of Gethsemane. Looking at that beatific portrait, I imagined he could hear what I was thinking as I sat there in front of him. Now that I think of it, I never really thought about what Mary would think. She was peaceful and serene, but I didn't think about talking to her. Jesus was the powerful one, and according to the painting, he was as beautiful as a woman and equally as compassionate and loving. I discovered while doing research for this book that I wasn't the only one who loved Mary. Anne Lamott writes in her book entitled *Plan B: Further Thoughts on Faith* that Mary is the feminine face of divine love.[1] Many of the women I spoke with while researching this book agreed with Lamott's statement.

---

1. Lamott, *Plan B*.

The story behind this book continues with another woman. Again, not me. The woman who enticed me to reconsider the Mary I remembered from my early years in the church is someone who would be a goddess in the contemporary sense: Olynda Smith, the creator of Wild Heart Yoga, and the director of yoga retreats that celebrate the feminine.

From the first moment when my car ground down the gravel driveway to a glassed-in building where women had started claiming their yoga mats on the sunny floor for Olynda's Devi Day, I knew I was in for something special. Her Devi Day celebrations are designed for women to enjoy a day of yoga and commune with each other, while learning more about the yogic philosophy. She offers insight into what defines a devi, a Sanskrit word for goddess, and personally, I believe she encourages us to recognize the devi within.

I spent an idyllic morning on the mats, gazing through the glass walls to the bucolic grounds outside, where fancy chickens clucked their stuff as proudly and loudly as the stately and glorious peacocks who make the place their home. Olynda offered teachings from Sarasvati, Lakshmi, and Parvati, the triad of Hindu goddesses, women who represented education and the arts and compassion. Their stories resonated with me and made me remember the other strong goddesses and women I'd read about as a child, when I haunted the shelves of our little neighborhood library. My curiosity was sparked. I wanted to know more. Much more.

Suddenly, I realized there'd always been a strong link between what I've believed spiritually and how those beliefs manifested themselves in my writing.

It made sense to continue.

To conduct research now, during this turbulent period in our history, is both empowering and humbling.

I've marched with thousands of women down the streets of our state capital, Raleigh, and it was entirely different from the other marches I've been part of or watched. To bring thousands to the streets means the cause is important to many more than just those who marched. And to be cocooned within a crowd that is 99 percent female made me feel loved, safe, and immensely powerful. The shining faces of the other women marching in front, behind, beside, and with me proved that we all believed we might yet have a voice. Those faces looked divine.

Four months later, I joined Olynda's Devi Day celebration again, but this time, I was the presenter, and I introduced the journal I'd created in a workshop called *The Divine Feminine* to a new group of devis, those goddesses. To create the journal, I'd dipped into the literature about the divine feminine persona, and I was hooked. I realized that what we extolled and celebrated in the divine feminine were characteristics that all people who identify as female embody, at one level or another. The only difference is that those elements are manifested by the divine feminine being in a state of perfection. We, on the other hand, are not perfect.

As I shared quotes and techniques that would open up the women in the workshop to a deeper level of journaling, I realized an urge to investigate divine women. I discovered that our ongoing global/political turbulence made me nervous—sometimes even depressed—and looking to the Divine helped me see that the power to maintain a calm in the storm around me was, indeed, within me.

Other women stated the same feelings during the workshop, no matter their religious or spiritual affiliations. It astonished me how healing it was to share our journals that day; it was even more so, when the women and I talked about the need to find something positive (and yes, divine) about themselves.

I wanted to learn more, and when I'm curious about something, I write about it. There's no better way to assuage my curiosity than to immerse myself in the research necessary to write with confidence about the subject matter. I contacted women from many religious beliefs and from just as many cultural backgrounds. I envisioned a book that would help each of us find our divinity.

Thus, this book began.

But why me? Why should I be the one to write this? I'm not a theologian or philosopher. I'm not a religious studies major. I'm not a historian, per se.

Here's what I am. I'm an academic who has spent her whole life researching the female experience, starting with reading every biography on my library's shelves, devouring every women's studies course in college, researching female writers and their voices in private writings and published writings for my master's thesis at Vermont College, and expanding on my analysis of the written word by studying transgender authors' voices, pre- and post-transition, for my PhD in the social justice program at Union Institute and University.

In my writing career, I have worked as a reporter and freelance journalist for national and international publications; I've written children's books about strong females like Beryl Markham, the first female pilot to fly solo from Britain to North America, and Edmonia Lewis, the first African American female artist to achieve fame as a sculptor. I've researched the art that women from a variety of cultures have created, and I wrote about them in my nonfiction books about African American and Native American arts.

One thing I have learned during the years I've spent being an observer of other women and a traveler who's exploring her own spirituality is that we all have basic needs, and the most basic of all is to be able to identify the self in a mirror. Our first connection with the outside world is recognizing our place within it, the philosopher Jacques Lacan states.[2] That vision of our self in the mirror cements our identity. In a sense, it determines our forward path in life. That mirror, however, is almost metaphorical. Sometimes that mirror is not a physical one, such as that metal-trimmed square above your bathroom sink. Sometimes the mirror takes a human form. Sometimes what is reflected is other people's opinions of your identifiable self. In a lot of cases, women's vision of their true self has not aligned with the way the rest of the world around them sees them. That is what needs to change.

All my writing and research has led me to an internal examination, pulling back the scrim of my own spiritual journey and how it has been informed by my writing and my thirst for more knowledge. Learning about goddesses and deities, about feminine icons who are powerful and who define their own philosophy and identity, excites me. The tales of the divine feminine are fascinating and empowering and eye-opening. I want to share them with you, and

---

2. Purdue University, "Modules on Jacques Lacan."

show you how these women, these divine entities, are an exaggerated version of our best selves.

The last couple of years have been tough for females. Events have ground us down, caused a general feeling of malaise, and I've heard women of every mindset talking about being depressed. The world around us split into many factions, so many factions that people don't know how to handle their personal interactions. But, on the bright side, women have realized that, when threatened, there's nothing more powerful than to link arms and take to the streets, celebrating the peaceful right to lift our voices.

So, that's who I sought: women who come from many different cultures and religions and philosophical backgrounds. I determined I'd reach as many secular women as possible, so I cast a wide net, relying on my friends and fellow academics to spread the word. Each of the people who volunteered answered the same questions, and as a result, ended up sharing their personal philosophical journey. Some of them were familiar with the term "divine feminine," while others had no idea what it meant. What they shared was the willingness to tell their stories.

Now, more than ever, is the right time to celebrate those goddesses and heavenly beings that have female attributes. It's time to embrace the Divine in ourselves, to delight in and relish feminine strengths, to recognize the goddess within.

How to Read This Book

This text is a conversation-starter between your public and your private personas. We all have lives we live in our heads, words we say in our minds that are never spoken, truths that we know but never admit to, understandings about our situation in life as feminine people that others will never understand. Your situation is different from mine. You will never find someone who's lived exactly the same life as you have with the same results. What I propose in this book is for you to see that, despite all our differences, there is one thing we all have in common: we've all traveled some kind of spiritual or religious journey. Think about your own, and about how that has influenced you.

Each of the chapters begins with a quote from a major spiritual leader or writer. This book will introduce you to a myriad of spiritual leaders that have been influential to me, as well as to the women I talked to during my research. Each of them is worthy of expanded study, and you are encouraged to do so by looking at the texts included in the footnotes, as well as the bibliography. Use this book as a tool, a stepping-off point for your own curiosity and your own spiritual journey.

I've included many of the divine beings/goddesses/feminine creatures from many of the world's religions and cultures. Because there are so many, I focused on the more recognizable goddesses or spiritual beings and grouped them in a way that aligns with the subject matter of each of the chapters in this book.

While you read, you will see that the divine feminine is referred to in many ways. In this book they are fluid descriptions and definitions: the terms woman/women/female include everyone who identifies as feminine. The terms will be used interchangeably.

Perhaps you'll discover what I did during my research. None of the women I spoke with are clergy or spiritual leaders, yet they all have had a very distinctive journey. I realized that is one thing we all share. We've all had a religious upbringing that we've cherished, or we've questioned. That spirituality is our personal divinity. Within us all is a divine being who has either questioned her path or celebrated it. Dozens of women either wrote extensive answers to my questions or sat with me, one on one, to dig deep into their belief system. Throughout this book, we'll explore the connection between what they've said and the historic models that I've gleaned through my research and my own personal journey.

That brings me to my final note about how to read this text: when you read any of my own stories, consider your personal journey. I've included pieces of my story, because our own narratives are what determine how we see others. My personal journey was the fuel that became this book. Each of the experiences either taught me a lesson or revealed something I needed to face in order to understand myself. I'm still a work in progress (always will be), but I wanted to share my own experiences to say that I'm there with all the other women who were willing to share with me—and with all of you. But you are the architect of your life. You walk a different path from mine (and from everyone else). So, as you read my story, think of your own. Keep a journal. Create a dream board. Ponder your own experiences. Know that, though the path you've walked has brought you to this moment, neither of us is finished discovering who we are.

Chapter One

Defining the Divine Feminine and Divine Masculine

Most godly energy has been defined as either masculine or feminine, but when you add the word "sacred" or "divine" to the definitions, you can see how those energies each play a role in how we behave.

It is common to think of an all-powerful male in the heavens when asked to name a sacred entity, a divinity. If asked about the sacred female, few equate that being, that particular divinity, with a goddess in the sky. That's a fact. It's also a fact that masculine energy is seen as powerful and overwhelming, while the feminine energy is seen as more calm and peaceful. But where is that divine feminine?

Brett Hargis, one of the women I interviewed, says it this way: "I wondered why there were no feminine influences in the church when I was young, but wasn't overly troubled with it. In college, I realized that I was out from under my parents' roof, and I could form my own opinions. I dabbled with other forms of worship, drawn the most to paganism, and the ability to choose one's own deities."

She didn't find the female form in her own church, so she searched other belief systems and found that face in the deities she could freely choose. In the range of philosophies and religions, there are divinities of every description, but as you will see, certain personality traits generally define the divinity as a god or a goddess. When the male and female roles are unbalanced in our human form, we experience what are often termed "psychological side effects." A person might have too much anger or might not be able to be creative or compassionate enough. One might experience the sense that only others who have spiritual cachet can "save" them instead of relying on their own survival techniques.

Thousands of years ago, men and women lived in an egalitarian society, where both the masculine and feminine were valued and equal. Yes, people were still not what we define in today's world as "civilized," but they were equal. A man's role was as important as the woman's. They worked together to survive. Jobs formed out of necessity, and personality traits were shaped by those "jobs." Necessities: feed self, keep fire, procreate, feed family. Jobs: hunter, gatherer, hearth keeper, educator of the children.

We still need to have love and family, we still need to eat and have a roof over our heads, and we still need to teach future generations! We cannot be just one or the other. Incorporating both the yin and the yang, the masculine and the feminine, is what works to create the balance in the world.

All of us have a mixture of masculine and feminine energies. I have a philosophy that we go through stages in our lives where these energies ebb and flow. I know I have distinctively masculine personality traits that I've struggled with through the years. Even though I had a strong mother who taught me to stand my ground, society's voice was even stronger, and early lessons I learned included not to rock the boat, even when I wanted to yell and scream about a cruelty I'd seen or experienced. On the other hand, I have choked back tears more times than I can count because crying is seen as a weak, "feminine" trait. I'm sure you can look at yourself and find a mixture of both energies, as well. I accept mine as part of my personal makeup now. I hope you do, too.

Those masculine and feminine energies became more defined once human beings began domesticating animals and exerting their power over nature; demanding their superiority, destructive energies began rising to the surface and people began to battle each other. In other words, when we began destroying nature, we also began the destruction of our own divine characteristics. The pendulum swung to the destructive traits (killing, consuming, dominating) and to counterbalance where we are now, we must embrace the divine feminine, creating lifestyles that are more likely to connect in a positive way with people, animals, and natural elements.

The divine masculine energy is that which relies on math and science. A person with this type of energy is analytical and rational, thinking with the left side of the brain, the side that leads to logical thought and determination. These types of people are courageous and fearless protectors, loyal to the core: leaders who aren't afraid to speak up, adventurous and fearless. The divine masculine seeks to provide, control, and protect. The tendency toward power can become destructive if that power leads to harmful force, war, or bullying, and ultimately it creates a violent society built on the need for one part of society to surrender in order for the other to live.

Conversely, divine feminine energy is intuitive and compassionate, creative and spiritual. It is associated with motherhood: both the divine motherhood, as well as the Earth Mother, and the Divine Self. Motherhood is defined as both by birth and by choice: a child that is yours via your womb, or a child that you have chosen to mother. It is a holistic way of thinking that results in an emotional response and collaborative way of working with others. Feminine energy tends to favor the personal relationship before the industrial. Feminine energy values the intimate and is nurturing and passionate. It's that intuitive feeling in your gut, the wisdom to sense and feel. The feminine/she gives birth to both people and ideas. She will love, guide, honor, and nurture you. The divine feminine embodies imagination and peace, passion and abundance, but if those characteristics are not whole, if the feminine energy is damaged somehow, the feminine can become desperate, apathetic, and powerless. (There are plenty of exceptions to the rule, but generally, this is how the feminine is defined and depicted.)

If people are able to combine both the divine masculine and divine feminine, they become balanced and able to communicate fairly, and to intellectually combine creativity, love, and compassion with logic and action. To have too much love and compassion can sometimes cause us to be naïve, while a lack of the same causes a person to become malicious and unfeeling. To have equal amounts requires attention and sensitivity in order to maintain balance, but I think there are few who would question the benefit of trying.

These traits aren't necessarily indicative of the person's gender. A female who thinks analytically about a problem and responds with a logical action plan is simply incorporating divine masculine thinking into her being. A man who responds to a sad story with compassion and understanding is using the divine feminine way of thinking. Both should exist within males and females in order to balance the personality. It's the balance of yin and yang, the puzzle pieces that create the whole circle. You must have white in order to have black, night and day to complete a cycle. Opposites are necessary in the world. Nature shows us that every day. A balanced set of both traits is best. If sacred energies combine in a healthy and equal way, there is nothing they cannot do!

I believe males tend to become more compassionate and intuitive as they age, while women tend to sharpen their analytical skills and become more competitive as they mature. That is my personal theory, because I've seen many examples of it in my lifetime. Perhaps it's because women are often single in their senior years (men often die before their spouses), or women might realize as they age that in order to accomplish what they must, they need to sharpen their linear thinking skills. In any case, it seems that we go through a natural balancing act in our lives. Some of us find that happy medium, the balance of the yin and yang, while others continue to search for it or to have problems even defining it.

Juliette Wood, author of *The Concept of the Goddess*, explains it this way, "Modern feminism provides the context for study of the Goddess in the last few decades. Within the context of religion, it has attempted to rebalance or redefine the relationship between male/female aspects of the deity."[3]

Even more important is that those energies—the divine feminine and divine masculine—have been out of sync for a millennium, and the only way we will help this planet, ourselves, and the rest of humanity is if they are in alignment. For example, when the divine feminine uses her love and wisdom to nurture and honor another, she creates a place of peace and support. When the divine masculine is employed, the person believes in him/herself, enjoys the adventure, and the exploration, and does no harm. The effect becomes synergistic and balanced. If there is any combination of energies,

---

3. Wood, *The Concept of the Goddess*, 9.

there must be a natural balance or alignment so that everyone finds comfort in the balance.

The other side of the argument is that the definition of the divine feminine changes depending upon who is offering their perspective. Whenever we are faced with a subject, we come to understand it through our own lens. What I mean by that is that our histories, every moment of experience that makes us who we are, bring us to an understanding of the world around us and how we define it. When we are faced, as human beings, with defining a philosophy or a theology, basically a belief system, we understand it through our own lens.

That could be a bit myopic, a pretty narrow view of a very wide and interesting topic.

I hope I can shift my lens a bit to show many other opinions and voices and definitions of the divine feminine—other than mine. So, perhaps I'm agreeing that the definition will change depending upon your perspective. That's fine. Let it be. Let's just all be women for a moment. Feminine-by-choice human beings. Feminine/masculine human beings. Just plain old human beings.

Reflection

An activist and award-winning writer, China Galland has been writing about finding the feminine face of God throughout her career, and her work has won her the prestigious Courage of Conscience award from the Peace Abbey. Galland is a professor in residence at the Center for the Arts, Religion, and Education at the Graduate Theological Union in Berkeley, California, where she directs the Keepers of Love Project.[4]

This quote describes that balance of female and male, dark and light. Galland claims that because Mary is the mother of God/Jesus, she is also God, because if she is the mother, she is the original creator since she came first.

Mary is also God: unacknowledged, female, and dark.

She is the Mother God. God, as I am using the term, is both what we describe as female and male, both dark

---

4. Galland, "About China Galland," https://resurrectinglove.org/about/.

*and light, and neither male nor female, nor dark nor
light, nor any other term that we can use.*

*God the Mother is just as real and present today as any
other human conception of a power which no human
term can fully describe.*
~ China Galland[5]

When you reflect on Galland's point as biological (kind of like "Which came first: the chicken or the egg?"), it makes sense, doesn't it? Or does it make more sense that God is the Mother? In any case, does that make God female?

Practice: Seeing into the Mirror

During this first practice, I feel it's time for you to look at yourself and see who you are, so find a mirror. (Go ahead, I'll be here when you get back.)

Set that mirror on the table or stand in front of that mirror on the wall. Stare at your reflection. Really look at yourself. Turn your head from side to side, up and down, lean forward, lean back. Who are you? Do you feel divine? You should!

Keep looking into that mirror. Stare into your eyes. Get close. See the beautiful brown/blue/green/black/gold in your eyes? Look deeper. See those black pupils? That's the edge of your depth. You are looking into your own soul.

As you're looking at yourself, say your name with confidence. Repeat it three times. You are that name and so much more. There is something inside the depth of your eyes. Stare into that something. What is it? See your power. Can you define it?

Five minutes is not a long time, but it can feel like forever when you're staring at yourself. I'm going to challenge you to stare for as long as you can—and find something positive about that image. Say it aloud ("I see determination in my face" or "I look like my mother" or "My eyebrows arch every time I laugh"). Find something good and say it (over and over, if you need to).

---

5. Galland, *Longing for Darkness.*

This is only the beginning. By the time we're finished, you'll be able to identify every goddess trait you own in that gorgeous face of yours.

Main Takeaways from This Chapter

- Definitions of masculine and feminine energies
- Discussion of analytics vs. intuition
- Learning to become more balanced
- Looking deeply inside

The Goddesses

Jiutian Xannu (Chinese), the goddess of war, sex, and longevity

Valkyries (Norse), twelve female figures who decide who lives or dies in battle

Deidre (Irish), legendary figure promised to royalty but in love with another

Bhagavati (Hindu) or **Devi**, the female aspect of Shakti (divine masculine).

Diana (Roman), goddess of the hunt and wild animals

Durga (Hindu), goddess of war, strength, and protection

Minerva (Roman) or Athena (Greek), goddess of handicrafts, professions, arts, and war

Joan of Arc (French), saint who led battles in Hundred Years' War

Justitia (Roman) or **Dike** (Greek), the goddess of justice

Ma'at (Egyptian), goddess of truth, balance, harmony, law, order, and justice

Chapter Two

We Are All Divine Feminine

Each of us embodies some of the characteristics discussed, whether divine feminine or divine masculine. We have all had moments of knee-quaking love and passion, of experiencing the heartbreaking events that bring a tear to our eyes, of responding to nature with a whole and full heart, and of realizing that our leadership might save others. We are all capable of offering our divine qualities to the world in order to save it and its people from civil unrest, to protect its religious freedoms, and to protect the environment from the years of subjecting it to damage we, ourselves, have inflicted. If we are women, we know that the secret of life itself is within us. Our bodies nourish, protect, and give birth to other human beings. After those beings begin their lives on this earth, we protect, love, and educate them. When those sacred elements are denied us by the patriarchal powers, life itself is denied. Though the sacred wisdom known by our forebears is lost (feminine wisdom was passed along verbally; masculine wisdom relied on written knowledge), we can reclaim our intelligence and understanding by being patient—which is another divine feminine virtue: listening and receiving.

In today's world, we need to not only remember but also to retain the sacred wisdom we once knew. We need to understand what we lost so long ago when the feminine was degraded, when the masculine culture stole the power by burning temples, and, yes, by also burning the people—women, mostly—who carried that sacred wisdom. While women suppressed their anger and suffered with fear, they also suppressed their own magic, their power.

Feminine knowledge is not something that is "New Age" or "cosmic," but instead is about the wisdom women hold of their natural place in the world, where the cycle of birth, death, and rebirth intersect. Mother Nature has taught us of that cycle and of the balance of light and dark, creation and death, pain and pleasure. We know that all the pieces work together to make the whole. It's not a religious type of knowledge or a lofty philosophy. The understanding of the earth's cycles is innately female.

The divine feminine understands how she is interconnected to her body, to the natural world itself, to those children to whom she gives birth, and to those people within her family of origin. She knows she has played the role of imitating the rational and scientific world and ignoring her own special knowledge of relationships and the patterns of creation. Those relationships are all part of the organic whole, the structures that work together to create a harmonious planet. It is the sacred connectivity of all life.

That "magic" understanding has always been there inside you. The mystery is quite simple, nothing to be afraid of and little that is suspect. We have simply forgotten our divine mystery, but it is there, within you, and all you need do is claim that divinity, create a sacred space where you can remember your true nature, and celebrate the powers that make you divinely feminine.

When considering the impact of women on today's religious societies, I discovered that the number of women in religious positions is rather low. For example, Tibetan nuns number more than twenty-eight thousand (compared to forty-six thousand priests).[6] In 2014, there were approximately fifty thousand Catholic nuns, a 72 percent drop from the late '90s, which is when the last census was taken.[7] Though women who hold roles in religion number in the thousands, few of them hold major roles in administration even now. In addition, though most religious leaders are men, their audience is largely female.[8]

Sara Noor, one of the many women I talked to when writing this book, said this: "The divine feminine, to me, means the attribution of powers to a feminine deity as in the religions of older civilizations. It also means a

---

6. Willis, "Tibetan An-s."

7. Pew Research Center, "U.S. Nuns Face Shrinking Numbers."

8. Pew Research Center, "The Gender Gap in Religion Around the World."

woman is the focus as a spiritual figure or leader contrary to male-centered religions … [the] 'divine feminine' constitutes certain qualities attributed to God like mercy, forgiveness, and creation, which have a ring of femininity to them, as opposed to powers like protector, provider, or destructor, which are stereotypically male. So, divine feminine for me is a female-centric approach to divine values and powers in theology and social aspects of life."

The Stages of Being a Woman

The triple moon has long been used to designate the triple goddess (Maiden, Mother, Crone), and many drawings from ancient times show the woman's body with the place of creation (the vagina/womb) as lit with magic light or a symbol of the never-ending circle of life. Archetypes exist in every culture, beginning with the oldest depiction of a woman that has been found, a forty-thousand-year-old, 2.5-inch-tall figure of a voluptuous woman carved from a mammoth tusk. The figure has been dubbed Venus of Hohle Fels after the area where it was found in Germany, and it is thought that the figure hung as an ornament around its owner's neck.[9] As soon as I saw it, I knew it might be the depiction of a goddess and that the person wearing it was probably a devoted follower. At that point in time, most of the world worshipped goddesses, but later, goddesses became lost in cultures. Some became identified as witches; others were feared or simply ignored or forgotten, their powers or abilities usurped or no longer recognized as valid. Instead of goddesses with incredible power, they became the Maiden, the Mother, and the Crone. I believe there is at least one more archetype that can be included in the stages of being a woman: the Warrior. Many goddesses are strong women, depicted with shields, spears, and swords, and paired with dangerous animals. We cannot ignore their place in the history of deities.

Miriam Schulman, one of the women I interviewed for this book, says, "I also believe there are divine energies, an area I haven't yet explored a whole

---

9. Coghlan, "Ivory 'Venus' Is First Depiction of a Woman."

lot, that are surrounding and supporting us at all times. These energies may include divine goddesses, as well as our foremothers and their foremothers."

I think she's right, and I also believe that we bring those divine energies with us and utilize different strengths at different times in our life. So, let's define the stages of female-identifying humans this way: Maiden (Virgin), Mother (Queen), Warrior (Matron), Crone (Wise Woman). These four stages cover all of the decades of a woman's life and celebrate the undeniable powers that every woman holds in the center of her being.

Maiden (Virgin): From her own birth until she becomes a mother, a woman is a Maiden. During this stage of her life, a woman asks questions and learns a little about who she is. As a child, the Maiden is full of life and energy, running and jumping, fully engaged in playing, and laughing often. She is introduced to the natural changes of her body, and hormones create havoc with emotions in her mid-teens. It is a time of gathering knowledge, abilities, and skills.

This period is often referred to as the spring of a woman's life, earmarked by discovering her sexuality and determining what course her life will start to take. It is a time when others take care of her and try to seclude her from that in the world which will hurt her.

Mother (Queen): Though this phase of a woman's life is continuing later than it did, say, a hundred years ago (when women married and had children at a younger age), and some women choose not, or are unable, to have children, the Mother phase is defined by the creation of life (let's call it "building a family"). Because of the fullness of a woman's body during the act of creation, this period is considered the peak phase of the female life cycle.

At this stage, often called the summer of a woman's life, women are sexual beings, commanding the attention of others around them, and are often considered seductive. Becoming a mother constitutes a sea change, and raising children introduces women to a more rewarding period when giving (instead of receiving) becomes the norm. Because of the attention paid to family, women at this age tend to forget themselves, and they might need encouragement to step out of the caretaker role and enjoy themselves again.

Warrior (Matron): When a woman is at the peak of her career and the babies are out of diapers, she is more likely to strike out on her own once again, often because of divorce or death, but sometimes simply by personal choice. Instead of juggling family duties, she is likely to enjoy her own life again, to travel, or to purchase a home of her own or to dive into a new lifestyle. This woman has traveled enough of life's road to know her own mind, and even though she might not verbally voice her opinions and feelings, she has definitely formed them. Ironically, at the time when she has the most freedom, a woman is likely to step back into the caring role with grandchildren or aging parents.

Crone (Wise Woman): A woman is considered a wise woman or crone when she is past the middle-aged mark, a time when she has finally balanced her work and home life, and begins taking more time for herself. It is the winter of her life when the ground is barren and there is less of life left than has already been lived. She might be moving more slowly, noticing the changes in her face and her body in the mirror, and accepting that she has few years left to enjoy. It's a thoughtful time when the woman goes deep inside to prepare for the inevitable end to the physical life. This is the time when she is most experienced, and with that experience comes wisdom, which she often shares with younger people, passing on lessons learned, and in many cultures, acting as teacher or leader.

There's a term that Zen practitioners use to describe a person who's very compassionate, who has a certain softness and a sympathetic heart: "old woman Zen."

Most women of this age report a rejuvenated love life as a result of having more time on their hands and no worries about becoming pregnant. I suspect that rejuvenation might also be the result of an increased level of self-confidence and self-worth. In some ancient cultures, post-menopausal women were considered to be like virgins once again and were charged with conducting sacrifices determined by sexual purity.

The Key to Life

There is no power greater than the power to create. I'm not talking about creating a book or a piece of art. I'm talking about the original act of creation: the creation of human life. Only women can deliver a new human into the world, and many female deities or goddesses are said to have been responsible for the birth of the world itself. From Australia's Yhi, who created the world when she first opened her eyes, to India's Devi, a power within all goddesses and a being who transcends all categories, the divine feminine of the world are responsible for the birth of the world/humans in almost every religion and on every continent. The ancient religions shared one commonality: the female deity was depicted as a sacred being who was as powerful or more powerful than the gods themselves.

When you are responsible for giving birth, it makes sense that you continue to take care of the being you created. Whether that being is human, another god, an animal, or even a whole world, the creator loves the creation (even when that offspring might be having a bad day). The original creator, Mother Nature, provides life to all the beings she has created. She provides trees for shade and homes, grasses for food and protection, a brilliant sun to warm the earth and to bring forth all that grows upon it, and a moon that gives us time to rest and holds in its power the movement of the tides.

Kenna Lee Fudge, one of the women I interviewed, said that she thinks "that the term 'divine feminine' is indicative of the wonder of the deeper, more traditionally 'feminine' qualities of mankind. It's exalting the inner characteristics that are typically deemed girly, bringing to light the beauty in being intuitive, kind, nurturing, strong, and caregiving. I would say that allowing myself to be divinely feminine would be like saying it's the other side of fierce."

First referenced in writings in Mycenean scripts as "Mother Gaia" in the thirteenth or twelfth century BCE, many cultures personified nature and the growing cycles as female, thus creating a divine feminine. Once the Bible became a text that early Christians followed, the strength of Mother Nature/ Gaia diminished. Since God was the creator of the earth and heavens, Mother

Nature or the Earth Mother fell beneath him since she tended to the earthly world rather than the heavens. Still, it's a power that still trumps almost every other goddess/god. Without nature, the world does not exist, and since Gaia/Mother Nature/Earth Mother is responsible for all things that grow from the earth and all beings who live on that earth, one could say she's at the top of the food chain. It is no surprise that she would be the first to be "demoted" when the patriarchal nature of the world began to assert itself.[10]

Today's World: Taking Back the Power

There's an old saying: "If Mama ain't happy, ain't nobody happy." That has been especially evident the past couple of years. For thousands of years, women have been the victims of abuse and rape, stereotyping and belittling, dismissal and indifference. In certain cultures, women are still stoned to death; in others, a woman might have acid thrown at her face simply because she is trying to get an education. Women still struggle to make the equivalent salary of a man doing the same job. We have learned through the years that speaking out about the abuse we've endured, the sexual humiliation, the gender discrimination, and the disrespect we've put up with on an almost daily basis is useless. We've learned to be silent—for the most part, because quite a few of us have bought the lie that we're alone, that we are weak, and that it's better to suffer in silence.

But something happened over the past couple of years that pushed women over the brink. More than thirty high-profile politicians, businessmen, and entertainers have been accused of sexual harassment or misconduct since 2014, and more appear in the media every day.[11] Multiple women are coming forward in each case. It appears to be the norm that these men have not only committed their crimes against one woman but against many. And once one woman comes forward, the others are encouraged by her bravery, and that one voice in the wilderness becomes stronger with every one that joins it.

---

10. Timeless Myths, "Gaea."
11. Corey, "A Growing List of Men Accused of Sexual Misconduct since Weinstein."

Those voices become thousands, marching throughout the world, wearing knitted "pussy caps," linking arms, and rejoicing in the sisterhood we share.

After those marches, women of every economic strata—women who work in grocery stores and fast-food restaurants, women who work in their homes, women who have put their own children on hold to take care of others, women who drive tractors or airplanes, women who teach and cook and create beautiful works of art, women who run businesses large and small—discovered each other and all that they share, even when there seem to be few similarities between their lives. Those women learned that the way to change what has made them unhappy is by banding together, arm-in-arm, and raising their voices.

It has begun working. Women all over the world have voiced their opinions about politics, have called their politicians to do their jobs in a way that benefits women, and they've raised issues that have long been swept under the rug because of fear. By joining together to battle for their rights, they have learned their power, they have conquered their fear, and their voices have been lifted to the heavens. The warrior goddesses—Jiutian Xannu, the Valkyries, Deidre, Bhagavati, Diana, Durga, Minerva, Joan of Arc, and many others—have given their hearts to normal women and those warrior goddess hearts now beat behind human ribs.

Call for the Goddess of Justice and Balance

Lady Justice originated as Justitia in Roman mythology and as Dike in Greek mythology, but she also exists in other cultures. In imagery, she is usually blinded and holds a set of balance scales, and her figure can be found on the edifice of almost every court in the world. Her blindfold signifies that it doesn't matter what the people look like or what their background might be; everyone she faces will get her swift and unbiased judgment, whether rich or poor, important or insignificant to the community at large.

The ancient Egyptians called their goddess Ma'at, and she represented the philosophy of cosmic order and balance. As long as there was balance in the world—as long as Ma'at represented law and order, truth and justice, harmony and power—there would be stability and order on earth. Since she ruled both gods and people, she was in charge of ensuring everything ran smoothly—particularly relationships between people: doling out advice, smoothing upset relationships, and keeping everyone following the rules. Just like a mother does.

Without the type of balance that Lady Justice and Ma'at keep in society, a portion of that society will always break the law and commit crimes, and another segment of the population suffers. For many centuries, women typically have been the victims, and I'm certain that those goddesses in charge of human behavior would not be happy to see the imbalance that has existed among the genders.

The call for justice to become balanced, as it should be, is ringing through communities small and poor, as well as through the gilded halls of government. Women see the goddess with her scales, and they know those scales haven't been balanced for a long time.

It's time for the goddess of justice and balance to shine brightly. It's time for women everywhere to believe they have the right for that balance and for justice. It's time to believe you have it inside; you have that divine right to call for justice. Yes, it takes time for that culture to change, but change has begun.

Trust: Lean into the Divine

The way to best recognize that you are the divine feminine is to trust in yourself. I say "lean into the divine," but perhaps the better verb would be to "fall" into the divine. When you lean, you still have some control over the distance you're leaning, and if the person/thing you're leaning against bends or breaks, you can still catch yourself. So, fall instead. Trust that the wind will still be there beneath your wings, that the strength you seek is already there within you. You have all that you need; just believe and fall into it.

The strength of the goddess is that she brings others close. Think of children who reach out to each other naturally. When I pass by local daycare centers, I see the kids hugging their friends as much as they can. The goddess is strong in children because they've built no walls. No one has convinced them (yet!) that they can't fly.

My Story: Finding the Women in the Library

I've read voraciously since I could put a sentence together. Everything in the library was fodder for teaching me my place in the world, but I always veered toward trying to find stories about strong women. There were a few: Amelia Earhart, Florence Nightingale, Annie Oakley, Joan of Arc, but compared to the stories about boys and men that occupied those library shelves, the books about women filled only a tiny corner.

During the summer months, I read comic books, looking for that female superhero that matched skills with Superman or Batman or Spiderman. Sure, the industry recognized that even girls read comic books (surprise!) and gave us Supergirl, Wonder Woman, and Cat Woman, but their skills never matched the men's, and none of them looked like any women I saw in our neighborhood or at school. None of our mothers had incredible breasts and tiny waists. No teacher stood, arms akimbo, taking up space, appearing to be at the ready to fly into the heavens. And of all the women I knew, none appeared strong enough to leap high in the air, holding a shield and wielding a sword. Perhaps the reason I found it difficult to find role models in these superheroes is because only 26.7 percent of all the superheroes created by the folks at DC and Marvel are female.[12]

I couldn't find superheroine role models because they simply didn't exist.

Yes, we had a Wonder Woman TV show; Cat Woman played a secondary role in the various Batman series; She-Ra and the Princesses of Power were popular in the '80s, then returned in 2018; and Supergirl was the focus of a couple of series, but again, their roles were subservient to the men, almost as though they were afraid to really rock the boat. I wondered where the women in charge were.

When I began writing for children, I remembered all those books about women that I read over and over again, because I couldn't find any new ones, and I wondered whose history I had missed. Surely, warriors and queens and powerful leaders existed. I wanted to write about them. Finally, I found the

---

12. Shendruk, "Analyzing the Gender Representation of 34,476 Comic Book Characters."

Candace queens of the Kingdom of Meroe, a powerful line of rulers who have been marginalized in the pages of history books. I dug them out, wrote about them, and sold the manuscript (only to have the publisher close). Because I was busy with other projects, I reluctantly filed that story away.

Then, several years ago, while recovering from surgery, I found a new TV show called *Game of Thrones*. I watched the first season, enthralled. The stories sparked that need to read about strong women once again, and I ripped through George R.R. Martin's books as if they were a box of Godiva chocolates.

All of the women in that series are warriors: from the virginal and rebellious Arya, to the righteous mother Catelyn Stark (and the bad mother, Cersei Lannister); the fire-defying warrior-queen Daenerys Targaryen and the knight-in-shining-armor Brienne of Tarth; the mystical woman Melisandre; the powerful queen-to-be, Sansa; and the wise and powerful crone Olenna Tyrell. They are all as powerful as the men—in most cases, even more so. Without these female characters, the story would have no forward motion.

I watched and realized that the divine feminine exists in every one of these women. Each is a superheroine in her own right and for different reasons than any of the others, yet they have undeniable similarities. Every female character in the show battles for her family, her lands, her loves, her animals. Each wears her goddess traits proudly, and even though those traits can be both positive and negative, there is one thing that is undeniably true: all are strong women. I don't remember ever watching a television program or a movie with such iconic female roles. It was thrilling—and they are amazingly powerful. We all have feminine and masculine traits, and once we understand that, we can see complexities and balances in fictional characters, as well as in reality.

These characters reflect the goddesses that have been part of each religion since the dawn of time. They inspire me the way Joan of Arc and Florence Nightingale did during those early days of reading every book on our tiny library's shelves.

Reflection

Ma-Tsu is a Chinese sea goddess (often called Mazu) said to protect the seas; she was the heavenly version of the shaman Lin Moniang (960-987 CE), and she is thought to have died while protecting her family from a typhoon. In Taiwan, as well as in other Asian countries, there is a major annual festival celebrating Ma-Tsu. Called many names by those communities who celebrate her, Ma-Tsu's role as the Heavenly Empress/Holy Mother/Grandmother makes her one of the major Taoist divinities. She's often depicted as coming out of the seas or standing on a water lily.[13]

This quote speaks about the final stage in a female life: the crone stage. That word has a negative connotation with people who feel that it denotes someone like the witch in Hansel and Gretel: an ancient woman with a hooked nose who can cast spells on those who anger her. I prefer the term "wise woman."

> *Don't return to your native town:*
> *you can't teach the truth there.*
> *By the village stream an old woman*
> *is calling you by your childhood name.*[14]
> ~ poem for Ma-Tsu

Though the image of the crone denotes age, this poem is a positive rephrasing that indicates that the knowledge learned throughout a life is valuable. Ageism is one of the most pervasive prejudices in our society, yet it is often not recognized as damaging.

As you ponder this quote, it would be a great idea to create a two-column list of how to recognize ageism and how to rephrase our thinking about women in their golden years.

---

13. Mother-God, "Divine Mother, Ma-Tsu."
14. McDermott, *Political Psychology in International Relations*, 82.

Practice: Breathe With Me

When you believe you've lost control of your life or would like to understand it better, the first and easiest step to take is to learn how to breathe. It's the easiest, most natural event in our bodies, yet we often forget that it's very easy to control.

So, let's practice by doing a breathing meditation.

Inhale a long and hearty lungful. Exhale to the count of eight. Do this three times.

Release your shoulders, loosen your jaw. Inhale to the count of eight, exhale to the count of eight. Say your numbers aloud.

Then finish this breathing exercise with three more deep inhales and exhales; if you are able, place your fingers to the ground beneath you. Feel that support.

Remember the woman in the mirror in our previous practice? She is all you need. Breathe her in. Breathe out your shared power.

Main Takeaways from This Chapter

- Defining feminine knowledge and wisdom
- Counting the numbers of women in male-centered religions
- Discussing the stages of being a woman
- Taking back the power
- Making the connection to the goddesses of justice and balance

The Goddesses

Mother Mary (Christian), the mother of Jesus Christ

Hestia (Greek), goddess of the hearth

Kuan Jin (Buddhist), goddess of compassion, mercy, and kindness

Lady Fatima (Catholic), saved the life of the pope

Mary Magdalene (Christian), first person to witness the resurrection of Jesus

Sarah (Christian), the mother of nations

Annapurna (Hindu), mountain goddess

Durga (Hindu), warrior goddess

Esther (Jewish), saved the Jewish nation

Hagar (Jewish), handmaiden to Sarah

Awitelin Tsita (Native American), earth mother

Nokomis (Native American), corn mother

Sarasvati (Hindu), represents wisdom

Minerva (Roman), goddess of war

Brigid (Irish), mother of Irish gods

Ch'ang O (Chinese), moon goddess

Hathor (Egyptian), mother goddess

Sedna (Inuit), goddess of the sea

Miriam (Jewish), biblical prophetess

Lady Godiva (English), patron saint of churches and seminaries

Saint Catherine of Siena (Catholic), doctor of the church

Ceridwen (Welsh Celtic), goddess of prosperity

Pele (Hawaiian), goddess of the volcano

Saint Quiteria (Catholic), protector against dog bites

Isis (Egyptian), goddess of the moon and protector of women and children

Athena (Greek), goddess of war

Medb (Irish), warrior queen of Connacht

Bhagavati (Hindu), the power beyond this universe

Chapter Three

The Feminine Face of God

Every religious philosophy recognizes female divinities or goddesses, beginning with the very first religions recorded. The feminine face of god embodies many personas, but the most common are the goddesses with connections to the earth. We've already discussed several versions of Mother Nature, but other types of earth goddesses are found in many belief systems throughout the world. Some are another type of mother: the spiritual mother. Divine beings such as Mother Mary (Christianity), Hestia (Greece), or Kwan Yin (Buddhism) are the goddesses that followers pray to for compassion, mercy, and forgiveness. But in today's world, India is the only place where such goddesses are still worshipped.[15]

Following the goddesses is an ancient spiritual path that has changed through the years, and before we discuss that a bit, let me clarify something. When I say that someone might follow a goddess, I mean that in the broadest of definitions. I'm coming at this subject from both a feminist and an earth-based spirituality, but I want to look at all the schools of thought to evaluate how women all over the world can embrace the divine feminine, and to see their differences and similarities.

In early civilizations, the male/female roles were reversed. Priestesses wielded power before their male counterparts, priests, did. Medicine women healed family and community members before medicine men. The traditions built by those goddess-based societies have been suppressed since then. The divine feminine qualities aroused suspicion and were cast aside as superstitions as Western cultures began valuing ambition over love; logic and

---

15. Harvey and Baring, *The Divine Feminine*.

strategic planning over intuition; the accumulation of physical riches over the "family, creativity and respect for the natural world."[16]

Little girls, like one of the women I interviewed, Tanveer Zehra, have vivid memories of the women they learned about during their childhood. Tanveer says, "I remember listening to stories about the Lady Fatima, the daughter of the last prophet of God. I have held her in the greatest esteem ever since."

I honor the goddesses in every religion: in Christianity, the divine feminine is represented by Mary Magdalene or Sarah or any of the many saints. Mary Magdalene, the first to see Jesus's resurrection, is considered to have received a secret teaching from Christ and is one of the Bible's women who is revered almost as highly as the men. Sarah, the wife of Abraham, gave birth at the ripe old age of ninety, and if that wasn't enough, God promised her that she would be the mother of nations. In Hinduism, the divine feminine is Annapurna, the goddess of food and nourishment. The mountain called Annapurna was named after her and is considered dangerous because of its unpredictable climate. Durga, a warrior goddess in Buddhism, protects all that is good and rides astride a lion/tiger, her many arms holding weapons that she uses to fight the good battle. Tara, also a Buddhist goddess, is divine, and to me, her image is both romantic and realist. She is called "she who saves" and fights like a mother for her children. As a mother myself, I connect with her. In Judaism, Esther and Hagar are divine, even though both were humans. Esther saved the Jewish people from destruction, while Hagar was addressed by God several times and was used as a handmaiden for Sarah. Hagar and her son Ishmael were saved by God as they struggled through an arid desert, which shows her importance in the biblical story. In Native American philosophy, Awitelin Tsita, the earth mother, and Nokomis, the corn mother, are both considered divine. Awitelin is a Zuni goddess, always shown as very pregnant, because she gave birth to every living being. The corn mother, Nokomis, belongs to both the Ojibwe and Algonquian traditions. She, too, gave birth to living things, but she did so from the ocean.

---

16. LaPlant, "2017—The Year of the Goddess Awakening and the Divine Feminine Returning."

The ultimate divine feminine goddess is the Earth, but she's also the personification of female deities celebrated and worshipped in every tradition. Hundreds of goddesses exist even in one single religion, and in each philosophy, there is an element or two that a goddess possesses that might also exist in me—as it does in you. I honor them all—and I honor whatever/whomever you might recognize (or if you choose not to recognize anyone at all). We all have our own journeys, and here, in this book and in my heart, all are accepted.

Women in education might favor goddesses like Sarasvati (Hindu), a deity who represents wisdom; or Minerva, the Roman goddess of war, who also was known as a patroness of the arts and wisdom; or Brigid, the mother of the Irish gods, who was known for her healing powers, as well as her love for poetry and wisdom. If you love gardening, saving the elephants, or bird watching, the Chinese moon goddess Ch'ang O, or the Egyptian mother goddess Hathor, or perhaps Sedna, the Inuit goddess of the sea, would fascinate you. For those who would rather look to those goddesses who walked on the earth, the Old Testament offers Hagar, Esther, or Miriam; you might be interested in the English Lady Godiva, who was the patron saint of a number of churches and monasteries; or maybe even Saint Catherine of Siena, the twenty-fifth child in her family (most of her siblings died since the family lived during the plague). She is considered the patron saint of firefighters, the United States, Italy, sexual temptation, and nurses.

You don't need to be a person who loves nature or children or the arts to find a goddess with whom to identify. Take Ceridwen of the Welsh Celtic faith, a goddess who is considered to be connected to prosperity; or Pele, the Hawaiian goddess of the volcano, who is known for testing the generosity of others. Neither are necessarily someone you'd want to emulate, yet we can learn something about ourselves from both of them. What about the warriors like Joan of Arc and Saint Quiteria (a virgin martyr of France and Spain), women who were inspirational and spiritual to the point of losing their own lives for their religion?

The author and archeologist Marija Gimbutas has written about the goddess culture in all of her books. According to her research, the mother-goddess culture dominated late Paleolithic religious beliefs. Women, themselves, ruled the culture.[17] And that's what I mean when I say you are the divine feminine: there are as many faces of the divine feminine as there are aspects of the human personality. Even countries or regions are depicted as feminine in the Bible. Israel is referred to at various points as daughter, bride, whore, queen, and mother.

Since following the goddess is an ancient path, it's not surprising to discover that the practice has changed greatly in the centuries-long history of religion. The stories of these deities/goddesses, the women who become saints, or those who are respected as goddesses in their own time often morph over the course of decades or centuries because the myths and tales of a culture's deities were told by the campfire. In other words, they were not written down. When tales of cultural beliefs and legends of revered beings are passed along from one generation to the next in spoken form, some stories change drastically, and some stories are lost completely. And to complicate that loose way of passing down the history of female deities, the stories might have been told by men, who may have decided not to continue certain veins of the story of the female face of god. In some societies, it became illegal (highly discouraged in others) to pass along the stories of Isis or Athena, Medb or Bhagavati.

My friend and one of my interviewees, Anne Bochetti, said, "The first thing I can remember hearing about the divine feminine was learning about the blessed Virgin Mary, who is, in my belief, the mother of us all, and because my mother's belief was so strong, she became a symbol of the Divine Mary because she lived her faith completely."

The Female as Defined by the Patriarchy (or How Men Created "Women")

Ella Disco, one of the women I interviewed, defines an exalted leader or goddess as one who should embody "the quality of divine justice, meaning not

17. Wood, *Concept of the Goddess*, 19.

justice through the legal system, but the spiritual justice among things—through compassion, nurturing, service, [and] kindness. Compassion: that we have a compassionate nature that doesn't get played out a lot in the news. Nurturing: these divine figures nurture the world. When you look at divine figures and you look at us, we are getting put down and the qualities are not seen as valuable. The things we do while mothering, what the mother does is important, and we've been doing that for the world. This, to me, is where we need to catch up and lay the foundation of these qualities in everything we do."

In the Christian religions, women have always been less than their male counterparts. In the beginning, the male God was the Creator. He was the one responsible for creating Adam, who then gave part of his rib to create Eve. She did not give birth. He did. But as the first woman, Eve gave birth to humans. She was the first mother. She was also the one blamed for the pain that would be inflicted upon humans from thence forward.[18]

As history moved forward, men controlled the world, and the stories told in the Bible informed Christian men and women about their relationships with each other and within the world. Tales are told throughout the Bible of women who supported their husbands, in ways that are very controversial by modern standards. Take Hagar, for example. She was commanded by her mistress, Sarah, to climb into bed with Sarah's husband Abraham, so that they could conceive and have the child Sarah was unable to give him. The descendants of Ishmael, the son Hagar would give Abraham, were called the "sons of Hagar." The name means enslavement to the Law of the Old Covenant, as written in Genesis, Psalms, and Galatians. Basically, Hagar was used as a sex slave, and if you have watched or read *The Handmaid's Tale*, you'll see a direct correlation. Ordering a maid to share your husband's bed isn't something I believe most women would be comfortable doing.

The Bible also tells the stories of women who were not Israelites or Christians, women I'd run into later on in my life, such as the Candaces, queens of the Kingdom of Kush, currently known as the Sudan (Acts 8:27). I researched them for a children's book and became fascinated by these women who ruled their kingdom without the help of a man. One of the Candaces led her troops

18. The Bible, Genesis 1:26-31; 2:18, King James Version; del Mastro, 51.

into battle, losing an eye in the skirmish; another is said to have had a relationship with Alexander the Great; and all were strong, legendary leaders.
The Candaces were worshipped as Egyptians did their monarchs, who were
also pharaohs, but current research is beginning to show that the Kushites
had their own distinct culture and religion, separate from that of the other
regions surrounding the Dead Sea.

To me, the Candaces are equivalent to another group of strong, ruling
women who held their own as protectors of the realm: the Amazons, who
appear to reflect the ways the patriarchy attempted to overpower a strong
women-centered culture. Though the Amazons are often misunderstood (the
comic book phenomenon has done a good job obscuring what is real and
what is comic fantasy), I do find great correlations between the Candaces and
the story of that most famous Amazon: Wonder Woman.

In Greek mythology, the Amazons were the daughters of Ares, the god of
war. It is said that they became a tribe of warrior women who lived near the
Black Sea in Turkey. Legend had it that they only visited men for procreation
purposes and often took those men as slaves. Several of their most famous
warriors are credited in battles, such as the Battle of Troy.

When the new *Wonder Woman* movie came out in 2017, I went to see
it in the theater on the first day. She'd been one of my role models when I
was growing up. I read every comic book featuring that Amazonian superhero that I could get my hands on. Yet I watched it anyway because, well, no
other superhero was like her. I learned then that any kind of superhero had
to have well-developed muscles and thin waists—male or female, but females
had one super power that males didn't. Wonder Woman, Catwoman, Super-
Girl, and BatGirl all had one thing in common: the majority of comic book
readers (and the majority of TV/movie aficionados) believed that the wom-
en's superhero ability was to defeat men simply by using their feminine wiles,
great bodies, and beautiful faces. But these women had brains, which is why
they were successful in defeating crime.

Seeing the movie as an adult gave me the opportunity to study the characters through a different lens—several, actually. I came away from the theater that day feeling strong, almost vindicated, because the movie not only

updated the Wonder Woman mythology, but it was a well-done flick. It was done with respect, but so many questions rattled through my brain that I found myself knee deep in mythology books in the library the next day. Where did this myth come from? Did this community of women truly exist outside the cheap pages of a comic book? Where had it gone?

After that immersive research, I knew much more about the legends of the Amazonian women through the stories told of them in Greek mythology, but what I didn't know until I started researching for this book is that there were several versions of the story, including one that puts the Amazons in Libya, making them African. Amazon women did not live near the Amazon River in South America. Some versions of the myths say that the Amazonian home was in a town called Themiscyra, at the mouth of the river Terme in northern Turkey; it was reportedly protected by a mist formed by Zeus. Ancient historians like Herodotus and Homer wrote of the Amazons, who were led by famous goddesses like Hippolyta (the goddess whose father, Ares, gave her a magic girdle) and her sisters Antiope, Melanippe, and Penthesilia. The writers told tales of the cities that Amazons had built; their reputation for being brutal in battle dominated Herodotus and Homer's tales. They shared stories of Penthesilea, who fought in the Trojan War and was eventually killed by the warrior Achilles.

All of these tales fascinated me. Here were women unafraid to fight for what they believed. Here were girls who ran and shot arrows and knew the strength in their legs and arms. Here were the females I was in my dreams.

The director Patty Jenkins brought the Wonder Woman story to the screen, but she did more than that: she brought the story to the world in a way that empowered women and girls, even appearing at the UN on the seventy-fifth anniversary of Wonder Woman's creation, prior to the movie's release. Some of the members of the UN didn't agree with Jenkins' suggestion that Wonder Woman should be an honorary ambassador because her character was not "culturally encompassing or sensitive" and that she tended to "objectify women."[19] It didn't seem to matter, since those women and girls who watched the movie loved the Amazonian women anyway. The film was a

---

19. *The Guardian*, "Wonder Woman Announced as UN Ambassador Amid Staff Protest."

box office success, one of the biggest films of the year, and the highest gross-ing superhero origin film to date in 2017.[20]

Before I sat down to watch the movie a second time, I thought about the Amazonian mythology and what it represented, about what it had meant to me as a young girl, and about how the strength of that group of females was a power equivalent to a man's. The Amazons wielded swords, shot arrows that always hit their targets, and rode galloping horses into battle. They went to war. Wonder Woman's power, though, was super-human strength, as well as a weakness akin to that of Superman's. If she lost her bracelets or if a man suc-ceeded in tying them together, she'd lose her powers. Instead of a sword or a hammer, she had a lasso that made those she captured tell the truth. She flew an invisible plane from one rescue mission to the next, and her tiara was as effective as a small missile when she hurled it at a foe. But the most powerful aspect of her personality is that she was the one who rescued men rather than vice versa. That, perhaps, was her greatest superpower: her ability to love and her desire for peace made her stand out from her male brethren.

The fact that this movie was the highest grossing of any film directed by a woman is enough of a feat to make Jenkins herself a contemporary goddess in my eyes. That kind of direct, "we're going to do it anyway," in-your-face proof that women have power in what they want to watch, how they want to act, and who they want to vote for, was never more evident than it was when Jenkins's *Wonder Woman* created box office history. She was the first woman to make a $100 million movie, a blockbuster by all standards. The movie also broke box office records and opened the door for other women to direct and produce huge movies (like *Captain Marvel*, which followed in 2019 and was directed by Anna Boden). Considering that women are in the minority in the movie business, Jenkins is actually the wonder woman here.

One of the other takeaways I found myself returning to time and again after the movie was that we see very few warrior women in stories on stage, on screen, or in literature. Those we do see tend to be fatally attractive in addition to murderous. I wonder whether that might be because beautiful women are

---

20. Guerrasio, "'Wonder Woman' Is Now the Highest-Grossing Superhero Origin Movie of All Time."

more likely to garner the viewer/reader's sympathy. Or is it that being a war-rior, in and of itself, makes the woman a mystery, and thus, enticing? I believe that someday we'll watch a movie about super humans, in which the female doesn't wear makeup, is not heartbreakingly gorgeous, and does not have a perfect hourglass figure. In other words, I await Hollywood's rendition of the average/normal woman who's the embodiment of the divine feminine. She is here, right now—in you and the woman next to you.

If, historically, the world was created by Mother Earth/Mother Nature/Earth Mother, then why would feminine traits like forgiveness and beauty and creativity and intuition and the ability to procreate suddenly be down-graded? Women are the creators. The first people to serve a divinity were priestesses. The first people to discover the powers of the plants and ani-mals that grow on this earth and to learn how to use them as medicine were women. The first doctors were women, yet in modern societies they are still in the minority in that field. However, the current trend shows that more women have been graduated from medical schools than men and a survey done by Athena Health states that "60 percent of physicians under the age of 35 are female."[21] The total number of male and female doctors still reveals a predominance of male physicians, but if this current trend continues, it won't be long before the medical field will be a female domain again, as it was cen-turies ago.

Many civilizations make note of women healers. One of the earliest his-torically recorded female physicians was Merit Ptah, who lived in 2700 BCE, and who has been cited as the earliest woman of note in the scientific com-munity.[22] Ptah's bravery is impressive, since any female caught practicing medicine in Athens at that time would be put to death. She might have been the first, but Ptah certainly wasn't the last female to put her life on the line and practice the healing arts.

Though a history of women in medicine will show that women have always been involved in caretaking at some level, a glance at the timeline for the history of medicine shows you that every major work written before the

---

21. M. Johnson, "The Healthcare Future Is Female."
22. Mark, "Female Physicians in Ancient Egypt."

mid-1800s was written by a man. As a researcher, I can only surmise that the reason women have not been more prominent in the medical field is because they weren't allowed to publish. Or perhaps they simply weren't allowed to be educated enough to even become medical professionals in the first place.

Historically, the major civilized societies of the world decided long ago that feminine powers were not worth as much as masculine ones and needed to be obfuscated. Religious wars ensued to obliterate the old goddess traditions. Women who had knowledge of herbs and the body, and were thus able to heal, became tagged as witches. All of their abilities suddenly became worthless. They became worthless. They became the enemy. The feared. But how and why?

Many of us now embrace the healing abilities that once condemned us. We burn candles and sage to clear our homes, we take vitamins and herbs for medicinal purposes, and we celebrate those who have the ability to read the body, all of which were skills women have known for ages. Still, the knowledge of women as goddesses often comes to us late. We listen and learn as children, but we question what we once accepted as we build our own lives.

"I was well into my twenties, before I came across Sue Monk Kidd's *Dance of the Dissident Daughter*, and it shook me to my core, the concept that the divine could also be feminine," Christina Sutcliffe, an interviewee says. "For a time, despite my tumultuous relationship with religion, I felt 'sinful' for even thinking of God as 'Goddess.' That book was the start of a spiritual transformation for me. It planted a seed in my mind, rooted in the concept that all the natural world was divine, all of us were included in a connection with our Creator."

Women who'd been midwives and able to offer birthing services to their community were burnt at the stake and effectively kept out of the field of medicine for hundreds of years. If a woman acted like an individual, if she were single longer than society expected her to be, or if she had knowledge that exceeded that of her male counterparts, she was suspected of being a witch and lost her life. If she questioned her father, her husband, her brother, or any other man, she was brutalized, beaten, or sometimes stoned to death. In some cultures, a woman was mutilated by acid or cut by a knife or razor. We still see aspects of this today, and the UN has a special division devoted to ending female mutilation, child marriages, and the general mistreatment of women throughout the world. Until there is no need for an organization to actively fight for these protections, women are in danger.

For thousands of years, men have held the right to correct their wife's/sister's/mother's behavior in whatever way they see fit. Women have endured centuries of physical, psychological, and emotional abuse. Thousands—perhaps millions—have died at the hands of a loved one. When they realized they might die, women changed their natural behaviors in order to satisfy the men.

As women began keeping to themselves, maintaining the hearth and the family, and acquiescing to the cultural standards, the qualities of the goddess started to change. The intuition most women experienced was stifled by the more accepted masculine qualities of logic and planning. Ambition became a more desired trait than love. Again, the masculine quality over the feminine. And family relationships, the arts, and nature took a back seat to the more masculine need to accumulate goods. In the masculine mindset, if women acted like women, they must amplify their weaknesses rather than explore their strengths, their intelligence, their abilities to heal or to create. Millions of fine minds and brilliant creators have been lost because of that shift, that devaluation of the traits defining the divine feminine.

Little by little, educating females became the norm, and by the mid-1800s, you can see a shift in the number of women with careers, as well as the number of women who were learning how to escape the cycle of domestic abuse. Their power, they realized, was in their words. Their voice. A slow, subconscious change began to take place. Women began to realize they could refuse the abuse, that they could choose to speak out. They began fighting back with their stories. Even if their physical power did not equal their attackers', they had words. It's been a slow, gradual change that continues this very moment.

Today, we're seeing a seismic shift back to the feminine. Here's one example: nunneries in Tibet are seeing an influx of women "queuing up for the privilege of training" to be a spiritual warrior. A religious leader, the Gyalwang Drukpa says, "We need women now more than ever. In this dark age, more female energy is certainly needed."[23]

So, what next? Is there a way that the feminine respect for the world around us can help heal what has happened to nature, to the oceans, to the vast world of glaciers, to the animals disappearing at brilliant speed? Can we solve the rifts between cultures by talking woman to woman? Can we come to a new respect of our own abilities and qualities of the goddesses?

I say yes.

Reflection

An American poet and playwright, Ntozake Shange is also a self-proclaimed black feminist whose best-known work, the play *for colored girls who have considered suicide/when the rainbow is enuf*, rocked the literary world in 1975. The poet Ishmael Reed said, "No contemporary writer has Ms. Shange's uncanny gift for immersing herself within the situations and points of view of so many different types of women."[24]

> *i found god in myself*
> *and i loved her*
> *i loved her fiercely*[25]
> ~Ntozake Shange

Shange encourages the divine feminine and self-love in this quote, a concept simple and "fierce." Why do you believe she repeats "i loved her" twice? What tone do you hear in these words? Do you love yourself fiercely?

---

23. Toomey, *In Search of Buddha's Daughters*.

24. "Ntozake Shange," *Poets*, accessed October 29, 2020, https://poets.org/poet/ntozake -shange#poet__works.

25. Shange, *For Colored Girls*.

Practice: Yourself in Others' Eyes

Time to surround yourself with the goddesses in your life. Think about the friends or family members who make you happy. Invite one (or a group) to tea or for a glass of wine.

When you share space and time with other divine feminine people, also share stories of your own female family members and friends. Celebrate the women who created their own herstories before yours. Talk with your friends/family about the women in your ancestral world. Discuss the personality traits that make you proud of those females. Do you see those traits in yourself? Do your friends' stories about their ancestors show the traits they might share?

Lift a glass to those friends/family, as well as to their female ancestors. Make that celebration a regular part of your life.

Main Takeaways from This Chapter

- Exploring the ancient spiritual path of the goddesses
- Offering introductions to some powerful, feminine divinities
- Discussing how man created woman all over the world
- Finding yourself in your own eyes

The Goddesses

Mother Nature (common), the personification of the world and all
  its powers

Kali (Hindu), goddess of rage and resistance

Oduduwa (Yoruban), mother goddess and original creator of the earth

Niamh (Irish Celtic), queen of the fairies

Demeter (Greek), goddess of the grain

Isis (Egyptian), cosmic mother

Athena (Greek), goddess of war

Mary Magdalene (Christian), first to see the resurrection of Jesus

Sarasvati (Hindu), goddess of learning and the arts

Chapter Four

Divine Traits

Which personality traits do you share with female divinities? Do you believe that any being who is designated as a goddess or god must have abilities that far exceed what you, a normal human being, possesses? Do you see divinities as perfect?

One of the questions I asked the women I interviewed was what character traits they believed defined a being as holy, sainted, heavenly, goddess, or wise. Jessica Emery probably said it best when she stated that the commonalities she sees among female divinities "are love, innocence, peacefulness, wisdom, and forgiveness."

Each answer shared similarities with the others, but there was one stark difference. Not one of the women said that a divinity gets angry. Not one. Yet there are powerful stories in the Bible about God's fearsome anger (Noah's ark is a good example), the gods and goddesses in the Greek pantheon are legendary for their earth-shattering rages, and even in the Hindu religion, Kali, the goddess of rage and resistance, is the Great Destroyer, even stronger than her male counterpart, Shiva. Surely everyone knows that you can't fool with Mother Nature, the most destructive mother in the universe.

So why wouldn't the women answering the questions admit to the power and rage and righteous anger chronicled in some stories about commonly known divinities?

My personal supposition is that language is getting in our way. The ways we describe the binary genders (male and female, for this argument) are indicative of the powers and weaknesses society has defined. A justifiable argument launched by a god/man at a dinner table becomes an embarrassing moment when a goddess/woman delivers the same argument in the same manner: raised voice, pointing finger, scowling lips. He's acting dominant, controlling the conversation, but she is a bitch, out of control, and she should be taken away from the table immediately. On the other hand, a god/man who pardons people who've betrayed him is thought of as soft and is often removed by those stronger than he, in much the same manner a lion pride removes a leader who can't battle the next strongest male. A goddess/woman who elects to forgive and forget is acting compassionately.

In our definitions of feminine divinities, we tend toward the positive qualities like compassion, forgiveness, caring, and love, all of which are powerful and strong, yet the words (powerful and strong) are not mentioned.

It's time we realize that it is harder to be compassionate, almost impossible to forgive, takes incredible strength to be a caretaker, and clear that the life-changing quality of love can resolve any issue.

That's power. And guess what? You all have it. Every single one of you.

As I conducted my research, I kept a spreadsheet for the goddesses I've researched, intending to examine where their attributes and "powers" may intersect. My list grew and so did my spreadsheet, to the point where it wound its way around my office when I hung it on the wall. Because the information and spreadsheet became cumbersome, I'll point out the most common traits attributed to female divinities, and I will note where in the world they are recognized and/or worshipped.

Approximately 75 percent of the deities are associated with nature, so it's natural that caregiving, understanding of the earth and its elements, and compassion are attributes that most of those feminine divinities share. That same majority of feminine divinities are also the ones with the ability to destroy everything they've built. They're incredibly powerful.

If you take care of your family and friends with the power of Mother Nature and the fierceness of a lion, you possess qualities of the divine. If you're compassionate and wish to help others, you're divine. If you're a gardener of any kind, you're reaching the earth with the same intentions that Oduduwa, the Yoruban mother goddess and original creator of the earth, exhibited. (By the way, the reason she was the earth's creator is because her husband was drunk and couldn't perform the act!)[26]

Some goddesses deliver lessons about communication or protect and inspire artists, while others are sexual beings who mate with other gods (and sometimes, humans) and are irresistible to men, like Niamh, the Celtic queen of fairyland. Those traits of being able to educate others, to communicate and resolve conflicts, as well as to honor one's own sensuality and earthiness, are all traits human beings share.

To inspire people who write, paint, make music, or dance is to fashion a creative universe, which is what goddesses like the Muses in Greek mythology purported to do. Human beings are the only ones (besides the goddesses/gods) who create art. If you're creative in any fashion, by writing, singing, dancing, quilting, sewing, knitting, painting, sculpting, or anything else that produces a piece of art, you are the divine feminine.

Early in human history, we see the divine female afforded the same respect as the divine male. Sometimes, even more so. After all, the divine feminine gives birth to some of those gods. Without her, the male god would not exist.

Demeter, goddess of the grain, is another mother archetype, and the Egyptian goddess Isis was worshipped as cosmic mother, god mother, and queen of heaven for more than three thousand years, ending in the second century CE. With the ability to heal the sick, she also exhibits the power to breathe life into Osiris, her heavenly husband. She's the lap/throne "from which Horus [her son] emerges and upon which he is seated."[27]

One long piece of verse entitled "Thunder, Perfect Mind," includes a stanza that is strikingly clear in its intent to show the power of the divine feminine:

> *For I am the First and the Last,*
> *I am the honored one and the scorned one,*
> *I am the Whore and the Holy One.*
> *I am the Wife and the Virgin.*
> *I am the Mother and the Daughter.*

---

26. Oxford Reference, "Oduduwa, Locked in the Darkness, in a Calabash."
27. Agha-Jaffar, *Women and Goddesses in Myth and Sacred Text*, 10.

I am the members of my mother.
I am the barren one and many are her sons.
~(author unknown, translated by G.W. Macrae)[28]

That piece of ancient poetry denotes attributes of the divine feminine that are repeated in other ancient texts as well, but are they valid today? The world is many shades of gray, and I, as well as others, no longer see gender as binary.

Recognizing and Celebrating Your Divine Feminine Attributes

I've offered an overview of those divine feminine attributes that are most common, but in the upcoming chapters, we'll discuss more and in greater detail. As you read, think about the varying divine traits and how they might apply to you. Remember that you embody the goddess, the divine, the holy, and the worthy. You are capable of great peace, as well as incredible anger. You have the wisdom to forgive and the compassion to care for others. You feel empathy for people. You are the peacemaker, the creator, the dream builder. You administer medicine, both from the earth and from your heart. You nurse animals and loved ones, and you know that your actions have a ripple effect that extends far beyond your front door.

You are connected to the mother, whether you reproduce or not, and when you can begin to understand the importance of that connection to the divine mother, you can then open up and recognize that tremendous power within yourself.

As in reality, not all the goddesses depicted in religious philosophy are benevolent or worthy of praise and worship. As a practicing Buddhist, it upset me a little to discover that in Tibetan Buddhism, "it is specifically the female gender of one of the demon species, the Srin that comes to represent both the spirit world in its entirety, and the demonic nature of the early

---

28. PBS.org, "Thunder, Perfect Mind."

Tibetans, in a founding myth concerning the Buddhist domination over the indigenous Tibetan religion."[29]

In addition, the Tibetan word for woman—*lümen* or *kyeman*—means "inferior being." Though most cultures have taught us to feel inferior, few come right out and define us that way. It is up to you whether you buy into that inferiority. I doubt that the Greek goddess Athena would have, since she was not born of woman but sprang fully grown from her father Zeus's head. I don't believe the Christian Mary Magdalene felt inferior, even though she was depicted as a prostitute, or that the Hindu goddess Sarasvati, who is worshipped by those in the arts and education, would be revered if her followers thought her inferior. If you understand that your attributes are strong, positive, and demanding of respect, you will command that response. You can immunize yourself from those who want to make you feel "less than." When you love the divine feminine inside yourself, you will be treated in a divine way.

The Taoist belief system is simple. It echoes a contemporary saying: "It is what it is." Basically, Taoism states we shouldn't strive to change anything we have no power to change. In other words, the only person you can change is yourself. It's a centered vision that is "essentially feminine, gentle, balance, dynamic, and wise."[30]

This statement is deceptively simple. It should be easy to change ourselves and our own outlook, shouldn't it? Well, it's not. Changing yourself and your way of thinking is one of the most difficult tasks that you can give yourself. Habits are difficult to break, and it's easy to slip back into them when faced with the same situations you've encountered throughout your life. However, if you keep practicing the change (one change at a time is best), it's guaranteed you will find the change you wanted to see in the other because that person is reacting to the change in you. Make sense?

Sometimes we need to remind ourselves what we would consider holy or divine. Isabella d'Cunha, one of my interviewees, says that such a being would have a "value for human life, discriminates not between genders, colors, faiths, and financial statuses. Someone who brings people together, who

---

29. Gyatso, "Down with the Demoness: Reflections on a Feminine Ground in Tibet," 35.

30. Harvey and Baring, *The Divine Feminine.*

does not break down in the face of adversity, and one who will stand up to any power (other than God himself), be it national or foreign."

Jean Shinoda Bolen writes: "Listening to the call of the goddess and god within you is particularly helpful when you are experiencing emotional pain or undergoing a difficult transition."[31] It's often easiest to employ practices that will help you when you need them the most. Women often find it difficult to drum up the strength they need when faced with tough issues. Though not all women successfully find the divine feminine in themselves and learn to love their strengths as well as their weaknesses, the ability to fight back means overcoming pain by making a change in yourself. Fighting back doesn't necessarily mean you have to hire a lawyer to battle city hall (as my mother used to say). Sometimes fighting back might mean just making the decision to live your best life and love yourself.

One practice that helps me connect with the goddess within is when I study photos of my ancestors. My pictures are old, sepia-toned or black and white, and several of them sit atop my altar in my bedroom. Some of the faces are ones I have never seen other than in those photos: my great-grandmother on my father's side, for example. Though she passed away long before I was born, her wide forehead and intelligent eyes offer me an attribute I recognize within myself. I've noticed that my friends who are connected to their spirituality usually have the same type of "ancestor wall." My friend, the artist Alyssa Hinton, has photos of her grandmothers in traditional tribal dance dresses. Another friend, Ella Disco, proudly displays generations of women on her living room wall—a collection she spent months curating. We revere those ancestral women, knowing they gave us our strengths, our smile, our artistic natures, or our ability to settle family arguments. They are the goddesses we listen to when we are finding life difficult.

---

31. Bolen, "Discover Your Signature Goddesses."

My Story: Herbal Remedies and Perseverance

Through the years, I've lived in rural locations where I've kept large gardens and have attempted to learn about herbs and their remedies. I've sat with friends at their kitchen tables, the woodstove blazing, our feet snug in heavy woolen socks, talking about planting lavender in flat fields or nurturing the basil plants we started the previous summer. I'm always amazed at how certain friends can identify mushrooms that are safe, and how others can determine the right time to plant certain tomato varietals. I know it's not rocket science, but these pieces of knowledge seem to come naturally to them. The wisdom that connects human beings to the earth, and the courage it takes to determine which plants are safe, which roots might be medicinal, what should be boiled, and what should be eaten raw took thousands of years to learn yet few truly recognize that education as worthy as a PhD in plant biology.

I met my friend Alyssa Hinton, an artist with Tuscarora and Osage background, through letters we wrote to each other while I was writing my first book on Native American art. Years later, I met her in real life when I moved to North Carolina, and we became friends.

A tall woman with full grayish hair she wears clipped casually atop her head, and a bright, welcoming smile, she is comfortable in her own skin, strong and determined, and a creative of the highest caliber. We talk about creativity, we support each other, we share the woes of being working artists, and we discuss family traditions.

At her tiny kitchen table one night over a vegetarian dinner that warmed my bones for days, Alyssa and I talked about natural therapies, the use of certain herbs, and the power of the medicine wheel. We sat beneath the photos of her female ancestors and discussed the characteristics that made each of them powerful in their own right. We talked late into the night about our own responsibilities as creative women and how those ancestors didn't have the same opportunities we have.

"If I don't go out and grab that opportunity by the throat, it'll pass right on by," Alyssa said. "We don't have a choice. We both have to put food on the table."

I nodded. We are both single females responsible for our own futures, and that often indicates to some that we are also responsible for producing children and grandchildren as well. But I would argue with that position, as many have before me. Many who identify as female do not have children, so the idea that women are only good for bearing children is a sexist notion.

Neither one of us will ever complain about having to put food on the table, even though we have our challenges, and that is an attribute we share with our foremothers. We dig deep for the strength we need, and we persevere.

Reflection

This quote from the story of Sky Woman, her fall to earth, her creation of North America, the birth of her two sons, and her connection with animals shows how diverse her powers are. There are many stories about this Iroquois mother goddess, including one that indicates she died in childbirth.

> *Then the woman stepped onto the land. She sprinkled dust into the air and created stars. Then she created the moon and sun.*[32]
>
> ~Iroquois Creation Story

In most religious creation tales, women are the ones who create the world. In this one, the world/land is created prior to the stars, moon, and sun. Sky Woman created universes. Plural. What kind of analogies can you make after reading this story? How do you plant your own feet into the earth beneath you?

Practice: Burning Sage in Your Space

Whenever I move or feel somewhat unsettled in my home, I burn a bit of a sage bundle (one of my friends makes lovely bundles with lavender, sage, and other natural ingredients she finds on her own land, but you can find sage sticks in almost every health food store). This ritual has roots in both Native American practices and ancient herbalism.

---

32. "Iroquois Creation Story."

The ritual of burning sage is determined by your use, but whatever the reason you burn sage, you will receive the added benefits the herb provides. It is known to clear space to make room for positive energies, and the herb also aids in relieving stress, helping promote sleep, and changing the ions in your air.

When burning sage, light the tip of your wand enough to produce smoke. I like to address the four directions (North, South, East and West) and to ensure that I sage each corner of my room. Sometimes you may need to blow on the bundle/wand a bit to produce the smoke, but be careful not to create fire. You can wave the smoke, be creative with it, or simply create your own ritual pattern of spreading the smoke. Once done, have a big shell or shallow curved dish to lay your sage bundle in so that it safely dies out. After twenty to thirty minutes, check your bundle to see that it's completely out. Then sit back and enjoy the positive energy you've created.

Main Takeaways from This Chapter

- Exploring the connection between gardening and Mother Nature
- Defining the creative and education muses
- Celebrating your divine feminine
- Connecting to positive energy

The Goddesses

Joan of Arc (Catholic), led soldiers into a holy war

The Candaces (Kushite), warrior queens of the Kingdom of Kush

Inanna (Sumerian), goddess of war

Kuan Yin (Buddhist), goddess of mercy and compassion

Aphrodite (Greek), goddess of love and beauty

Vajrayogini (Tantric/Buddhist), prime deity in Tantra, the essence of all Buddhas

Chapter Five

Accepting and Embracing Emotions

One of the women I interviewed, Fizza Imitaz, believes that people "are human beings at first, and later we are divided into genders or sexualities to play our social and private roles." My personal belief is that each of us embodies the divine feminine, no matter who we are or how we identify. There are so many representations of the feminine, the goddess, and the sacred throughout world philosophies and cultural history that it makes sense that one of them will depict an aspect of your own personality, probably one you've thought of as respectful or admirable but not applicable to you. For example, historically, males led armies against other males. If we've heard of women who led their armies in what they considered a holy war (i.e., Joan of Arc or the Candace queens of Kush), they are the exception rather than the rule. That militaristic, firebrand, fearless, powerful female soldier is often depicted negatively, as is the wicked stepmother (instead of calling her the strong matron); the corporate bitch (instead of using the term the successful executive); and the cold and calculating surgeon (instead of tagging her the genius with a knife). The point is that women in power are often made to feel "less than."

I'm asking you to look at depictions of goddesses like Inanna, the goddess of wars, who was defined in Sumeria as a multi-powerful being who represented fertility and sensuality as well. To me, that combination of being a war goddess as well as one who's recognized as a being connected with sexual love is almost an anomaly. Usually, one who battles isn't also connected with sexuality, but when you think about it, that push-me, pull-you situation exists in both war and sex, doesn't it?

This goddess is complicated. When she evolved into Ishtar, her role expanded to protect prostitutes. Because of those roles, the people who worshipped her probably included temple prostitutes. Ishtar enjoyed great popularity, especially in the ancient Middle East, where other local goddesses and their roles became directly connected with her. Later tales of Ishtar call her the Queen of the Universe.[33]

This is a perfect example of the way the positive (fertility) becomes the negative (prostitution). A divine feminine would embrace both the fertility as well as the sexual aspect of this goddess, believing both to be equally positive and respectful.

The divine feminine emotions are important to the equal balance in our personalities, both male and female. To every yin, there is a yang; black and white are both necessary for the color spectrum; much of the animal kingdom needs both the male and the female of the species to survive. Your life will never be completely miserable or completely happy, but somewhat equal parts of both. Accepting and embracing the positives and negatives, the up and the down, the right and wrong, means we are balanced.

Carol Gilligan, one of the first feminist theorists I read in college, discussed the changes women experience during their lives, from the way adolescent girls become silenced, losing their spirit and ability to share their truth, to the point in their aging years when some of the feisty spirit comes back ... sometimes. Far too often, the silenced female who's afraid to speak out to the males in power stays quiet and invisible until the end of her life. Basically, the woman dumbs herself down, keeping opinions and thoughts to herself. Although some of us are willing to buck the convention and speak up, the truth is that being silent is what we're taught to do.

In Greek mythology, the woman Philomela was a victim of sexual assault at the hands of Tereus; so that she would remain silent, Tereus had her tongue cut out. Though she couldn't speak, Philomela wove her story into a tapestry that she gave to her sister, Procne, Tereus' wife. To punish him and to exact revenge for her sister, Procne killed her son Itys and served his boiled head to Tereus.

That didn't go over well, and when Tereus went after the women with an axe, they called on the gods to save them. The response was that all were

---

33. Britannica.com, "Ishtar."

turned into birds: Philomela was turned into a nightingale; Procne became a swallow; and Tereus, a hoopoe. The fact that they could all fly away safely leads one to assume that the gods gave those women the gift of freedom. Yet Tereus, who became a hawklike bird, could have been given a more painful lesson that would convince men to stop abusing women.

Sue Monk Kidd substantiates Gilligan's points that women didn't have a voice from the lessons she learned in the Bible. The men are the ones who seek God and have adventures, while the women "support and wait for them." It's true that there are few women mentioned in the Bible, and those who are, are generally supporting characters rather than the ones who are strong, knowledgeable leaders. It's easy to become a victim when you're trained to be submissive and to believe that men have all the answers, as well as the power.

Becoming the divine feminine you are means accepting and embracing the emotions and personality attributes that make you who you are. For some of us, that means trotting out emotions that are often considered negative. My interviewee Brett Hargis says, "I feel that women are often discounted as less than men who have the same or even less training than the women. Men are seen as the ones who don't flinch and can make the 'tough' decisions. I think that's a load of bollocks. Women are seen as more emotional. I think that's a boon, not a detriment."

Take, for example, the women elected to public office during the past decade or so. Now, here's a disclaimer: whether you're a fan of these candidates or not, there was a clear bias shown to the men running for office. Until just recently, women in public office didn't have much of a support system, no real mentors to teach them how to be empowered and to take control in situations where women are in the minority. A strong, tight-lipped response from a woman still causes some to react negatively. When Hillary Clinton ran for office, polls revealed that she was more positively viewed when photos in the media showed her smiling and looking upward. If her face was serious or the camera caught her in mid-stride through a fervent speech, the photos were used negatively. Conversely, the photos of the male candidates, and in particular, Donald Trump, rarely showed a smiling face. Instead, the men wore dour, often threatening, expressions, yet the language used to describe them is decidedly less negative than Ms. Clinton's descriptors.

We are taught, subliminally and otherwise, to cover up "negative" emotions like anger or jealousy. A man who swears at the car in front of him is having a bad day; a woman who uses the same obscenity not only raises eyebrows but is often seen as crazy or uncontrolled. Perhaps these seem like small differences, but the majority of women have learned to temper those emotions that are normal and expected in a man's behavior.

Many of our divine females are best known for displaying emotions attributed to feminine energy. For example, one of the most recognizable feminine deities in world religions is Kuan Yin, the Buddhist goddess known for the ideals of mercy and compassion, and for her ability to understand and care for all who have female concerns, particularly childbirth and child rearing. She is the only Chinese Buddhist goddess who is loved rather than feared. The emotions she represents are probably the most "female" of all that exist: love, mercy, compassion, understanding. Most antique shops, garden stores, and furniture galleries sell figures of Kuan Yin: a thin, graceful woman; almost otherworldly; usually in a seated, cross-legged position; her hands folded in prayer or held in the same open-palm hand mudra that Buddha is often depicted as using. Sometimes she has many arms, all reaching out to the sides to make a perfect circle. And she's also depicted in a casual seating posture, one arm resting on an upraised knee, supporting herself on the other elbow. She is a peaceful, benevolent figure of Mahayana Buddhism descent, combining both Buddhist and Chinese virtues, and is recognized and revered by many of the same people who follow Buddha. She espouses peace and encourages love.

In the Tantric philosophy, Vajrayogini is the goddess who makes the most mundane of moments or actions into sacred ones. She is often called the red, female Buddha, and her inner red fire reminds her followers that they have what they need within themselves. Her power is supreme, and one reason she has been dubbed the Buddha for our time might be that she has a simple message, yet she's the one who's easiest to reach when one needs help.

Are you the person your family turns to when they need assistance? Whose door do they knock on when something has gone wrong? Are you both strong and available, like Vajrayogini?

Other religions also have compassionate divinities, and the emotions they stand for are often shared by those who follow them, modelling their own lives after those divine feminine. For example, Catholic nuns' orders are determined by the type of work they do: teaching, contemplative, or service. All of them share the same belief that being pious and humble are the best qualities to have when serving their Lord. Their goal is to help others recognize and celebrate Jesus Christ and God, the Father, as well as to help and serve the order and the community within which they do their work.

Yet, even though, historically, we have these saintly examples of female divinities and holy people who inhabit places of respect in almost every religion in the world, we still do not fully understand or respect the female figure in any major religion. Some of the smaller religions do celebrate the feminine, but the majority of the world's religions do not. It seems to me that the reason is a human one. We lost our trust in the divine feminine when the patriarchal, agrarian society took over, but times have changed, and I do believe that the feminine beings on this planet are in the process of rewriting what's been considered "weak" or "less than." It's time to embrace your own emotions and welcome them with open arms rather than trying to hide them so you can be acceptable to others.

Sometimes I wonder how we accept and embrace the emotions we have rather than hiding them. One of the exercises that works for me is to write down my thoughts in a list; then I follow that with a list of the emotions I'm feeling. I compare them and ask myself whether they match or intersect, then I check in with my gut. If I feel flutters or an upset stomach, I sit with that feeling. Listen and follow your heart. Emotions are a source of goddess wisdom. Honor your emotions. All of them.

Interviewee Christina Sutcliffe says, "I feel that celebrating the feminine in culture will empower the feminine in culture. With that said, I feel I should mention I don't feel we celebrate the masculine in culture. Men throughout history were as children who thrust themselves into roles of full responsibility. They stumbled trying to establish 'laws' to govern, to protect—and in the process they found their roles gave them power, power they didn't want to share. So, they subjugated anyone who was 'other'—including women. The masculine 'clique' has been culturally guided across the globe to also exclude artists, intellects, 'heathens,' homosexuals, the weak, the malformed ... to the point where men have backed themselves into a corner."

The most intense emotion that humans experience, and which appears to have come from the goddesses, is love. No goddess embodies this emotion more than Aphrodite/Venus. As Botticelli's painting depicts, she is said to have been born from the sea. The goddess of love, desire, and beauty, Aphrodite is "the body's happiness at being alive."[34] The creative arts (poetry, music, art) celebrate her existence and power to inspire creative energy.

Aphrodite's ability to deliver all the special emotions that humans crave threatened Christianity, especially since that philosophy has denied sexuality and ecstasy, preferring instead to keep women under sacred authority. Instead of being honored as the goddess of love in our contemporary culture, she is instead blamed for sexual compulsions and the sadistic and vulgar responses to the natural bodily needs.

My Story: Understanding and Communicating

Throughout my life, I've purposefully tried to sit in the background, preferring the quiet, wallpaper form of communication. I like to watch people, listen, pick up phrases and actions for my stories. I truly don't like being in the center of things, yet I am always thrust there, and at one point in my career, I gave in and became the leader everyone wanted me to be anyway.

---

34. Harvey and Baring, *The Divine Feminine*.

There was a running joke in several of the colleges where I've worked that no one ever really volunteers; they're all "volun-told" to take on the chairperson role of a particular committee, or to head the meeting, or to lead the group. If tasked with a responsibility, I'll get the job done and by deadline. That certainty must have been clear from the get-go because it never failed that the job fell into my lap. Unfortunately, no one had ever taught me how to manage people, and managing people in a business setting is totally different from being a mother or the head of a household. Taking care of people you love requires one thing: love. Simple. Directing staff members and colleagues, encouraging them to do their jobs and play well with others requires skills that are usually taught to people who work together on teams. The only teams I was ever part of were the ones where one person was pitted against another: dodgeball, tag, Scrabble. I had no clue, so I turned to people I knew who'd taken management classes in college while I was learning Shakespeare, and those people were all men. Every single one.

Three men in my life taught me valuable lessons about being the leader of a department or college division. One was my vice president at Keiser College in Florida, a big, football-player-sized guy with a heavy Southern accent, a dark golf course tan, and the chuckle of a car salesman. Peter hired me after I moved to West Palm Beach to get married.

Peter knew that I'd taught before and had held some leadership positions, but I don't think he realized that I did not instinctively know how to lead. What I knew how to do—and quite well—was to follow instructions, and I followed his to the tee.

"Make sure everyone's in uniform, on time, and that the classes are running properly," was my edict from him. He instructed me to be outside in the mornings when students were coming to class, to make myself visible, and to ensure that faculty followed their syllabi. I did everything Peter told me to do, and he continued to teach me.

Then one day, for a reason I don't remember, he caught me in the staff kitchen and told me that some of the students told him that when they heard my footsteps coming down the hallway, they were intimidated.

"You don't have to act like Hitler!" he growled, his face red.

I was appalled and turned on one heel, making a beeline for my office, where I cried behind closed doors.

That night (and many nights over many years after that), I turned to men (both friends and family) for advice about managing employees. One piece of advice I've remembered is that you should not be friends with your employees.

I listened, and I learned, but it never made complete sense to me. Years later, when none of those men were in my life any longer, I realized that if I acted as they suggested, I didn't get the response I wanted from my faculty. I realized that the reason their advice didn't work for me was because I didn't have the same experience growing up. I'd never played on a sports team, never had a leadership role in school, and when I wanted to be competitive, I had been teased for it. They hadn't been. They came from a totally different place than I did.

What Peter and my other mentors taught me was the traditionally masculine way of supervising: all punishment and no support. Their edicts didn't come from a feminine spirit, which was what I needed, and for the most part, that's what most of the faculty I supervised needed, as well. I didn't toss all their suggestions, but I did put my own spin on them. I managed my faculty in a way I wanted to be managed. I respected their talents, encouraged them to use them, and taught them what I knew. If I had to negotiate or mediate, I did it in a softer manner. If I had to smooth feathers, I tried to keep my voice level, my hands in my lap, and an understanding expression on my face. Often, with permission, I'd hug those I spoke with before they left my office, and I like to believe I was firm but fair.

I wasn't a perfect dean/supervisor/manager, but by incorporating some compassion, understanding, and an ethical attitude, I encouraged and inspired people to "do good" or to at least "do better." I've asked both faculty and staff (as well as students) to bring their best to the table and to realize that no one is perfect. There are times I've had to deliver an edict or a consequence, and I remember the men who taught me, but through the years of developing my own style, I've realized that I only feel uncomfortable when I'm in a position of conflict. I've also realized that combining that compassionate side with a reasonable edge is what works for me, a balance of the feminine energy with the masculine.

Reflection

This quote is a bit different from the others I've included in this volume. I chose to keep this one, because in the Taoist philosophy, Doumu is actually the "Mother of the Great Chariot." She is defined as being both wife and mother of the god of heaven (Tian), thus she both rules at his side, as well as having given birth to him.

> The Tao is the breath that never dies.
> It is a Mother to All Creation.[35]
> ~Tao Te Ching

Being the mother of all creation is a pretty powerful position in the world, wouldn't you say? The ultimate leader. In spite of the incestuous implications in the relationship between Doumu and her male counterpart, Tian, this particular deity controls everything on this earth (and the Big Dipper!). If you are both creator and partner, you have ultimate control, right? Or does it mean you must share? It might be worth spending a couple of minutes writing about this thought.

Practice: Embrace Your Own Heart

"Listen and follow your heart" is cliché, but let's flip it on its axis. Let's think of this intuitively, dig deep into our most feminine selves, and look at the heart as a metaphor for who we are. Ours is the heart of the family, the one who provides unconditional love, who cares for others—both human and not, the one who is open-hearted and compassionate, seeing all life as sacred, and trusting her intuition. We are whole and divine when we are in touch with our innermost selves. When a woman's connection to her heart has been

---

35. Resonant Mind, *Tao Te Ching*, Verse 6.

broken, she doesn't trust herself to thrive. If our hearts are broken, we can't function. We can't live. We fold and die, figuratively and literally.

So, here's a practice you might follow. Sit still, feet flat on the floor, hands on your heart. Listen to your breath, and as you breathe in and out, count to eight on the inhale and eight on the exhale. The sound of your breath is like the ocean, coming in and out, a continuous flow. While you're breathing, realize that your breath will continue, just like you will. Know your body will support you, and call on your favorite goddess for love and protection. She is part of you as surely as that heart of yours. Cherish your heart and yourself. Recognize whatever thoughts come up and keep breathing. Your emotions are all valid and so are you. That broken heart will heal with time. Let the goddesses help you.

Main Takeaways from This Chapter

- Talking about women in power
- Defining emotions as a strength
- Channeling the male and female emotional attributes

Chapter Six

Divine Relationships

Many of the world's major religions have a creation story, evoking the beginnings of the world. Most of those stories show that a woman is necessary for the creation of not only another being, but of the world itself. In some cases, that woman became impregnated and gave birth by herself, and in others, there was a man or a god who had placed the world's seed inside her. In almost every case, that woman was as important or more so than her male counterpart.

I grew up with the Adam and Eve story, knowing that God placed the two of them in a compromising position and tempted them to break his rules and, ultimately, to bring forth the first human union. Eve got the blame for the temptation, yet it has always appeared to me that an all-powerful God would have had the ability to control that union. Be that as it may, that story, or one very similar to it, occurs in many other religions, often with a different perspective.

In Pawnee mythology, the union of Pah (the Moon God) and his partner Shakaru (the Sun Goddess) produced the first human being. The creator god, Tirawa, responsible for putting Pah and Shakaru together, became the first Native American matchmaker. As a result of this match, the first man was born, but Tirawa wasn't done. He went on to match the Evening Star and the Morning Star together in order to produce a daughter. After Tirawa did his god-matchmaking, humans populated the earth, according to Native American mythology, as Adam and Eve did in the Bible.[36]

In another Native American story, the Inuit believe that Aakuluujjusi is the mother of all creation. Unlike the others, she didn't need a man to help her out. Instead, she created people out of her clothing, as well as the animals

---

36. "Pawnee Creation Myth."

The Goddesses

Maya (Buddhist), Buddha's mother

Virgin Mary (Christian), Jesus's mother

Isis (Egyptian), goddess of love, fertility, resurrection, and magic

Allat (Arabic), fertility goddess

Pema Chödrön (Buddhist), Buddhist nun and writer

Tara Brach (Buddhist), psychologist, author, meditations

Mother Teresa (Catholic), Albanian-Indian nun and missionary

Marianne Williamson (Spiritualist), self-help author and spiritual leader

Ruth (Christian/Jewish), great-grandmother to the biblical David

Hera (Roman), goddess of marriage and fertility

Saint Adelaide (Catholic), patron saint of abuse victims, parenthood, and family issues

Saint Agrippina (Catholic), patron saint of thunderstorms, leprosy, and evil spirits

Saint Angela Merici (Catholic), patron saint of the sick, disabled, and physically challenged

Amaterasu (Shinto), sun goddess

The Candaces (Kushite), warrior queens of the Kingdom of Kush

Bathsheba (Christian), biblical mother of Solomon

Deborah (Christian), led the army of Israel via commands from God

Cleopatra (Egyptian), queen celebrated as both human and divine

Esther (Jewish), biblical queen married to Persian King Xerxes I

that Inuit needed to survive in their sub-zero climate. From the beginning, she took care of her people first, establishing that all-important female personality characteristic of being a caretaker.

Vari-Ma-Te-Takere, the mythical mother of all in Polynesian mythology, created six children—three were plucked from one side of her body and the other three from the other side. Her name itself translates as "the very beginning," meaning she was the first of all. The children became gods and goddesses, some of whom were hybrid beings (half human/half fish). Like many other myths, there are several versions of Vari's story, but one thing that all the stories have in common is that she is recognized as the great mother goddess.

In the Hindu religion, Parvati is the mother goddess of all, the wife of Shiva and the goddess over all the other goddesses. Sometimes she is confused with other goddesses in Hinduism, which is probably because the religion espouses reincarnation. However, that is not the discussion in this book. Since we're talking about divine relationships here, let's see how divinities are connected and where the female divine fits into each religion.

Parvati is always at Shiva's side and is considered his equal. She's also the mother of the important Hindu gods Ganesha and Kartikeva. She is one of a trinity of female divinities in Hinduism, sharing the "honors" with Lakshmi and Sarasvati. It's easy to become confused when studying Parvati since she has more than 108 different names and each of the other goddesses is a reincarnation of her.[37] Simply realizing that she is the Divine Mother is enough for our purposes.

Parvati's role is to destroy evil and bless her worshippers; thus, she is well known for being loving, as well as aggressive. To me, she's the original mother lion fighting to protect her cubs. I know plenty of women who share Parvati's traits, even though they might not know a thing about Hinduism.

The story of creation in Buddhism is different than others because, quite simply, there isn't one. In some Buddhist sects, there are creation stories that are fairly scientific in nature; none of them involve gods or goddesses who create the world and its inhabitants. One of the best books to define this

---

37. Ramesh, "1000 Names of Goddess Durga-Devi Parvati."

belief is the Dalai Lama's *The Universe in a Single Atom*, if you'd like to study this aspect further. The book is pretty heavy, covering quantum physics, consciousness, genetics, and cosmology, all in relation to Buddhism.

Buddhism does indeed address the feminine, but not as we expect. Instead, it is to note that in the teachings of the dharma there is no masculine or feminine. In another respect, there is change in Buddhism, constant change, and some temples now hold images of the Buddha that are both female and male.

Buddha's mother, the queen Maya, died seven days after giving birth to him, and is often not mentioned simply because there's not a lot of information about her, but we know this for sure: she was not a goddess, and the Buddha himself was a human being, though an extraordinary one. There are, however, stories that Maya existed as a goddess after her earthly death. Like other religious stories written by humans (including the Bible), we depend on their versions of life. One such story about Maya is that she came in goddess form to Gautama (Buddha) when he was near death, and she was distressed, as any mother would be. The story goes that Buddha comforted her, telling her not to worry because he will soon be a reawakened being. Consoled, she retreated to her heavenly abode.[38]

Other such stories (as well as different ones) exist about Maya, but perhaps the most important fact about Buddhism that we need to remember regarding the divine feminine is that there are many schools of thought within the religion, yet one fact remains the same: everything is everything. In other words, the divine feminine is not necessarily female, nor is the divine masculine necessarily male.

It's interesting, because during my research I expected to find a more "enlightened" aspect about the feminine in Buddhism, yet many times, I was surprised to learn that women aren't necessarily on the same level as men, other than that they can give birth to those who might (like the Buddha himself) find enlightenment.

---

38. Garling, "Three Forgotten Stories about the Buddha's Mother."

"The Buddha extols the joy for a daughter who is wise and virtuous but especially for the likelihood of being a mother of sons," and, as in most stories about mothers of great gods/kings, a woman who gives birth to a spiritual being must herself be divine.[39]

In many religions, women have fought to follow their own beliefs. Ella Disco, one of my interviewees, grew up in Christianity but chose to follow the Baha'i faith in her adult years. She says that "one of the major tenets [in the Baha'i faith] is the equality of men and women, so on everything we think about, every committee we try to put together, women are part of the decision-making process. There are many, many women who died for this very reason. One was a young girl named Mona, who actually kissed the noose before they put it around her neck. She was the youngest of nine women that were killed because of their Baha'i beliefs. 'You can kill me,' she said, 'but you can't stop the emancipation of women.' They killed her." In another part of the world, goddesses were often more visible than their male counterparts. Before 3000 BCE through the second century CE, Isis was celebrated throughout Egypt and northern Africa and throughout the Roman Empire. Temples and statues were raised in her image until Christianity spread throughout the region. After that time period, the Virgin Mary replaced Isis in popularity, and even those shrines that once held Isis celebrants now opened their doors to Christians who praised the Virgin Mary.[40]

Isis's story (written by the priests of Heliopolis) is that she was the daughter of the earth god Geb and the sky goddess Nut. Married to the Egyptian king Osiris, she represented motherhood, mourning, and healing. The priests told stories of how she helped the Egyptian people learn how to create textiles, make their own bread, and brew beer, but the most important part of her story appears to be how she rescued her husband, who was trapped by his brother, Seth, in a wooden box and thrown into the Nile. Not only did she find Osiris, but after Seth hacked his brother to pieces, Isis put him back together (except for his missing penis!)—and nine months later, gave birth to Horus.

---

39. Paul, *Women in Buddhism*.
40. Harvey and Baring, *The Divine Feminine*.

Many stories of virginal mothers and wives bear the divine feminine traits of building strong families, and a good majority of those women faced lives of difficulty. Manoah's wife, a barren woman who was unnamed in the Bible, was told by an angel that she would have a son, Samson, whose hair should never be cut. This story from the Hebrew Bible's Book of Judges never names the wife, though she held the responsibility of raising a recognizable and important biblical judge.[41]

There are also many women in religious history who are known for representing fertility, including Allat, a fertility goddess of the pre-Islamic Arabs. One of a trinity of desert goddesses, all three the daughters of Allah, her followers worshipped a white stone cube as her image. Depending upon which regional story you reference, she and her sisters were either daughters or consorts of Allah, and they are mentioned in the Quran.[42]

I interviewed Susanne Kalejaiye, who stated that "until women obtain their fullest potential, men will also be denied realizing that they, too, have a much greater potential, because men and women are like two wings of a bird; if one wing is weak or the feathers clipped, then the bird itself cannot fly." To me, this means that males and females need to work together to be successful.

Women in other religious philosophies report on their freedom with various levels of sensitivity. "Muslim women should feel privileged," interviewee Naqeeba Zafar says, "since Islam gives them every right they need to have. But in a society like mine, the belief system seems to be a separate entity. Patriarchal society has adapted the doctrine in its own favor, hence women's right of freedom and so many other personal choices are being ruled and suppressed since the belief system is determined mostly by men."

---

41. Book of Judges, Hebrew Bible.
42. Britannica.com, "Al-Lāt."

Dependence, Independence, Interdependence, Caretaking

Now that we can see the familial connections the goddesses/divine beings had with their consorts/husbands and children, it's easy to see how the family web was woven and the roles these feminine deities played within the family, as well as in the community around them. Some mother figures are directly related to gods, some are individual, and some are married to/have a relationship with human "husbands." Some give birth to other gods/goddesses, some to human beings, and some to ideals.

Most of the divine feminine beings have an undeniable independence, yet they also weave a web of interdependence, both with family members and the community and the natural world around them—just as we all do. There's also a type of dependence that fosters a deeply positive and commanding sense of caretaking that has incredible power. That ability to care for another being is one that is believed to be intrinsically human, but we can see from these brief stories about divinely feminine beings that the aspect of caretaking starts in the myths/legends/stories about the first godly women in our shared religious histories.

When a culture relates to a creation story or to a tale about powerful beings who rule human lives, that iconic tale is one that influences everyone. If the divine is a caretaker who will fight to the last breath to save a family member or lover (as Isis is said to have done), that becomes the role model others are expected to emulate.

In some religions, the divine female and divine male are so in tune with one another that they are said to be the same person. For example, the love between the Hindu woman Radha and her beloved god Krishna was so strong that the Bengali saint Chaitanya was said to have been a reincarnation of both lovers: Krishna on the inside; Radha on the outside. Or, as quoted in *The Complete Works of Sister Nivedita*,

> *God became Krishna and Râdhâ—*
> *Love flows in thousands of coils.*

Whoso wants, takes it.
Love flows in thousands of coils—
The tide of love and loving past,
And fills the soul with bliss and joy![43]

The physical embodiment of the Sarasvati River, the Hindu goddess of learning Sarasvati created an interdependence in many ways. Said by some to be the wife of Brahma and by others to be his daughter or even his grand-daughter, this spiritual being celebrated in the Vedic culture shows up in creation myths. Sometimes she is created by Brahma from a stream of water; in other tales, she is the tongue of Vishnu. No matter which tales are told, there's a sense that she is not only part of the river but part of the educational impulse in every human being.

A true metaphor for interdependence is the Greek goddess Hera. The queen of the goddesses, Hera is the goddess of marriage; she selects a partner wisely, and her identity might be closely aligned with that partnership. To her, marriage is sacred. Often jealous and vengeful, she was particularly aligned with women, protecting them in their maidenhood as well as in their marriages, and especially during childbirth. To me, she is the epitome of proof that a woman can be both independent and interdependent.

Though I'm sure jealousy is not a trait you want engraved on your tombstone, you can surely understand why Hera would be jealous of the many love affairs her philandering husband, Zeus, had with both humans and other goddesses. If your belief in the sacredness of marriage was upended, I'm sure you would be jealous, too.

The Feminine in Communities

Women cannot be priests in the Catholic Church, yet they can be sainted. The number of Catholic priests in the world hovers around 410,000 (give or take a few thousand), but Catholic nuns/sisters only number around 75,000, according to several reports, one of which was released after a major meeting

---

43. Vivekananda, *Complete Works.*

with Pope Benedict XVI.[44] The number of female saints is debatable, because even the Catholic Church itself does not have accurate records from the beginning. Catholic.org lists 784 females who were sainted; another source states that 80 percent of the saints are male; and yet another states that there are approximately 1,700 saints, total.

I point to saints in this section because these women are human beings elevated to a demi-goddess station in the Catholic religion. Most of the female saints worked within communities, earning their status of sainthood by their lifetime history of compassionate deeds and selfless acts.

For example, Saint Adelaide, born in Burgundy in 931, is the patron saint of abuse victims, parenthood, and various family issues. She married and lost her first husband, then became chattel for her husband's successor before finding her passion in life, which was to establish many monasteries and churches. She was an ordinary woman with horrible family problems, yet her belief in her religion spurred her to greatness. She was canonized in 1097.[45]

A perfect example of the historical mistreatment of women is Saint Agrippina, who grew up in a good Roman family but was beheaded during the persecutions run by Emperor Valerian. Recognized as a pious person in the community, her body was taken to Sicily by three devout women and given a proper burial. As a saint, she's the patron of abuse victims, parenthood, and family issues. In August, the city of Boston holds a festival to celebrate her.

Saint Angela Merici's story is an interesting and moving one with strong connections to her community. Named the patron saint for the sick, disabled, and physically challenged, Angela held a vital position in her town of Desenzo, Italy. She opened her home to the girls of the town, became their teacher, and led them into the Catholic faith, but she didn't stop there. She founded several schools, both in her own town and others, and her lifelong commitment to teaching others led her to travel throughout the southern part of Europe, almost unheard of for a nun in the early 1500s.

Catholic women are not the only ones in the world who have made a tremendous difference in their communities. Throughout the world, women

44. Glatz, "The Number of Priests Declined for First Time in Decade Vatican Says."
45. Catholic.org, "St. Adelaide."

create an impact on their communities in much the same way as these saints: by teaching, caretaking, protecting the victims, and becoming the religious conduit for those wishing to serve.

That's powerful stuff.

Anyone who has worked at the grassroots level in a community knows that in order for a community to thrive, it needs to have at its core a set of people who can pass along knowledge, care for the community's physical well-being, and create a foundation for spirituality. Human females who act in those roles embody the traits I've already discussed as divine. Without this type of support in a community, the people do not flourish.

Women have a pivotal role in those communities, as Christina Sutcliffe notes. "I have been an arbiter for peace in my family. I have served as mediator and middle person in my parents' divorce and a voice of peace in many family arguments and disagreements. In that, I have been a 'healer' because I sought to heal the rift in my family."

Despite the strengths that women bring to a community, the majority of the world's cultures are patriarchal, and in some communities, women still are not allowed to own anything without a man. If she is orphaned or widowed and childless, she loses everything. She is dominated by the men in the culture, forced to either marry or remain under her father's roof, not allowed to do much of anything without the patriarch's permission. In fact, it wasn't until 2018 that women in Saudi Arabia were allowed to drive their own vehicles.[46]

Many biblical passages refer to a woman's stature, such as Deuteronomy chapter 25's Law of the Levirate Marriage. According to that passage, if your husband died, you were ordered to marry his brother. Or, take for example, another passage in the book of Deuteronomy that states a husband can go outside the marriage, but if the woman does, both she and her partner will be put to death (Deut. 22:22). For those who take the Bible literally, these laws still apply. And for women who live under this type of patriarchy, the community becomes smaller, sometimes including only the woman's family members. The woman's life is constricted by the laws of the larger community.

---

46. Specia, "Saudi Arabia Granted Women the Right to Drive."

If young female-identifying people in any community learn at the knee of the older feminine role models, they become stronger, and when women become stronger, so do families, and as a result, their neighborhoods, their towns, their countries, and finally, their world. Who wouldn't want a world built on compassion, intuition, caretaking, and knowledge?

My interviewee and writer-friend Melissa Seligman says that when she was growing up, "[i]t felt very much like women were not meant to be considered 'heroes' or any kind of someone to look up to. They were mostly the ones who got 'men into trouble.' As I got older and converted to reform Judaism, it was a very different experience. Eve was considered smart and intelligent, not evil. Women were to be listened to and could be leaders. Women like Eve, Miriam, Sarah, Esther were not only strong, but leaders who saved men. That was certainly something I could get behind. I am not even sure how they look. It seemed their physical attributes became secondary to their abilities."

If there are women in the community to whom others can turn for support, the network knits people together, empowering them to care for themselves, as well. Considering that 70 percent of the world's 1.3 billion poor people are women, according to CARE, providing a social structure, respecting cultural traditions, and encouraging personal relationships are paramount. Empowering the feminine doesn't diminish the masculine. It breaks down barriers and results in women finding ways to challenge whatever stands in the way of a healthy and safe life. As CARE says, equipping women with the proper resources means that women will have the power "to help whole families and entire communities escape poverty."[47]

Women as Leaders

I'm sure we can all name one or two women who, during the course of history, led a country or a people to great success, even though they don't fill history books. Pretty low numbers, especially when women have outnumbered men for quite a while. Let's take a look at a few of the divine feminine

---

47. Care.org, "Joint Gender Community Statement on U.S. Foreign Assistance."

women and how they led, as well as some of the contemporary women who are considered leaders in their own divine way.

Amaterasu, a Japanese Shinto sun goddess whose name means "(that which) illuminates heaven," competed with her brothers (Susano'o, god of sea and storms, and Tsukuyomi, god of the moon) and lived in the heavens with them, becoming wife to Tsukuyomi.[48] A tale is told that she and her husband fought because he killed Uke Mochi, the goddess of food. Amaterasu was so angry that she separated from him forever, thus the sun and moon would never be together again.

This doesn't necessarily make her a leader, but I'm including her in this section because it is believed that the royal family directly descended from her. Since they are the leaders of the Japanese world, it's important to know that Amaterasu's power to shine her light on the world is metaphorical for the power of the royal family, who can also "shine their light on the world" as regents.

Other cultures in the world point to early female leaders and the ways they led the people in their sphere. For example, in the Tibetan culture, there is proof that at least one group of women resembling Amazons exist in areas bordering Tibet. A society that may have been Tibetan is described in the Sui shu and the T'ang shu as being matriarchal and matrilineal. The supreme ruler was the queen, and sons took the family name of their mother.[49]

This is unusual since there are few matriarchal societies in the world during the time of the Sui dynasty (518–618 CE). In fact, of all the societies in the world, there are very few that are matriarchal. One of my favorites is the Nubian society of northern Africa, in which strong female rulers created a society of ruling queens during the century before the birth of Christ. Called Candaces (some spell the term Kandake), this set of warrior queens ruled a world that competed with Rome and Egypt for their territory. They are mentioned in the Bible in the New Testament and one of the queens is said to have fought Alexander the Great.

---

48. Cartwright, "Amaterasu."
49. Gyatso, "Down with the Demoness."

In the intro of *All the Women of the Bible*, del Mastro points out that the women in the Bible are all "real women,"[50] thus another reason to believe that we are all imbued with the divine feminine attributes that Mary Magdalene had or even some that might be attributed to Bathsheba (wife to Uriah the Hittite, then wife to David, and mother of Solomon), a woman who might not be termed divine, since she is often depicted as alluring and arousing lust in King David, who arranged for her husband Uriah's death so that the king himself could marry her. I argue that Bathsheba does, on many levels, possess goddess-like personality traits. She is as sensual as Aphrodite, bearing five children, one of whom died. She was admired for her creativity and her patience.

The brave Deborah is an important leader; she commanded Barak (the son of Abinoam of Kidesh) to resist Sisera, the commander of the Canaanite army, part of the tribes of Israel. She was also said to have commanded men. Barak resisted her leadership and hesitated to accept her orders, but because her commands came from God and were prophetic, she ultimately led the Israelite army to success. Her life was celebrated with a hymn.

Cleopatra is another female celebrated by her people as both human and divinity. A leader, sensual woman, and creator, she has fascinated us from the beginning. Through the years, history, legend, and fiction have blurred to create many different versions of this queen, a mortal whose people believed to be a goddess, but one thing is certain: she led the Egyptian people with ingenuity and learned to align herself with powerful men, whom she manipulated in order to gain footholds for her people during a spectacularly tumultuous time in history. She believed herself to be a divinity, and she maintained control over the Egyptian dynasty. With her as leader, her land became the richest nation in the Mediterranean during a time when Rome was the dominant power in the world.

Esther (or, in Hebrew, Hadassah), from the Bible's Book of Esther, was a Jewish queen, chosen as a bride for the Persian King Xerxes I solely because of her beauty. Little did her new husband realize that he was also getting a

---

50. DelMastro, *All the Women of the Bible*.

heroine who would foil an assassination attempt on him, and who would ultimately save the Jewish people by asking the king to save her life, as well as that of her people. He grants her request, telling her she can instruct the Jewish people to defend themselves. They fought back against their enemies, killing thousands, but saving themselves from the complete destruction they would have faced, had it not been for Esther's pleas. Jewish people celebrate the feast of Purim in her honor.[51]

I would love nothing better than to continue this list, looking both backward in history to those women who paved the way for whole cultures to move forward, as well as forward to a time when the number of feminine-identifying leaders in this world at least equals the number of masculine-identifying ones. I envision a completely different world when that happens, a world in which communities are just and fair to all who live within them, compassion is more highly-valued than marksmanship, and life of any kind is honored.

Evolved Beings

Let's talk about the definition of the *evolved being* for a second. Though there are some philosophies that define evolved as being equivalent to existing in another dimension, I think there's a rational and reasonable definition for this term upon which we can all agree, across cultures, religions, and gender identifications. I believe that someone who has evolved has changed—substantially. I think evolved beings learn to see all sides and to calmly and patiently listen to any arguments presented to them. I believe they think deeply, accept freely, and understand far more than the average person. To me, Pema Chödrön is an evolved being, as are Jane Goodall, Tara Brach, Mother Teresa, and Marianne Williamson—you may find your list includes very different people. There is definitely room for more evolved beings at the table.

When I think about who has evolved or reached the highest sense of being that we can achieve as humans, I place greatest respect in those humans who

---

51. Britannica.com, "Book of Esther."

consider the greater good rather than the individual, and who have been able to learn more and to teach more than others might have. Some might be surprised that I've included Jane Goodall in that list, but as we'll see in the next chapter, women have incredible skills with animals, a sense we strongly tie to many of the divine feminine already mentioned; being able to understand this world's animal community is primary to our own survival. She knows how interconnected we all are and offers the world a unique perspective into our delicate environmental balance. Not only can she impart that knowledge to the standing-room-only crowds anytime she tours, but she does it with an intelligent compassion and is one of the kindest and smartest women I've had the pleasure to both hear and study.

Tara Brach, an American Buddhist, is well known for her meditations, both in book form and recorded. I've included her in this discussion about evolved beings because her work delivering meditations, lectures, and classes has helped many people find the way to peace. She covers topics such as racism, pain, grief, compassion, and anger.

Marianne Williamson might be best known for her run for president, but before she got into politics, she was famous for her self-help books and workshops on spirituality. A Jewish woman who has strong connections to Jesus, she has extensively researched religious beliefs and has delivered many speeches about the intersections of religious philosophies.

I've named contemporary people, but the evolved being can refer to those who have come to the very pinnacle of their belief and devotion to their religion: Buddha, for example, as well as Muhammad, Mary Magdalene, Bahá'u'lláh, and Jesus. All are human beings who immersed themselves in studying humans and their relationship to their god. All are human beings who delivered a message of peace, love, and understanding for your fellow human beings. Yet all of them, human beings who suffered as a result of their beliefs, continued to deliver their message in spite of personal dangers. They were our greatest teachers—and many of their first teachers were women.

My Story: Women Helping Women

Throughout the beginning of my life, I took my female relationships and friendships for granted, knowing that they were essential for my survival, but also just expecting them to always be there. My female family members would always be on the other end of the phone, my friends would have lunch with me on a Friday afternoon, my colleagues would share tips on how to connect with mentors or agents or editors—almost all of whom were also female. It wasn't until recent years that I realized how strong my bonds with my feminine friends are.

When my last novel, *The Mourning Parade*, came out in 2017, I threw everything in my arsenal into preparing the book for the world. I took out loans, I hired a marketing team, I bought a beautiful sign and all kinds of marketing materials, I had a book trailer professionally shot and edited, I blogged on Facebook, I organized a book tour that spanned the whole country, and I invited everyone I'd ever known in my whole life to celebrate the book with me.

It was a gargantuan task, but when I finally took a breath about six months after the book hit the shelves, it dawned on me that every single aspect of the process was dominated by women. All of my friends sat around my kitchen table with me and shared a bottle of wine and pizza one night, addressing invitations to the launch party. We did it again to address more than six hundred postcards sent to people all over the world. The launch party itself wouldn't have worked without the help of my sister and her best friend, or without the introduction from one of my strong female writer/friends. Then there's the trip across country. On every stop I made during the month-long tour, I stayed with a lifelong friend, a former student, a member of my family, or an old friend made new—all women. The people who welcomed me into their shops, libraries, and book clubs: yup, women. My editors, publisher, videographer, marketing person? All women. I can count on one hand the number of men involved in the process.

Why am I telling you this? Because the experience was magical. I felt like I was buoyed up on a double cloud of support, as though all those friends, colleagues, family members had joined hands, making an unbreakably strong net, passing me along from one to another, filling my heart with their love, and empowering me to do something I would not have been able to accomplish without them.

The power of women helping women is indescribable. Harnessing that power and embracing it can change lives.

Reflection

In this passage from the Bible, Boaz announces his new wife, Ruth, one of five women named in the genealogy of Jesus. She is known for her kindness and compassion to her mother-in-law, Naomi. This passage comes from the fourth chapter where Boaz and Ruth wed, and David's lineage is detailed. Ruth, not a wealthy woman, is thought to have been average in looks as well. What Boaz loved about her was her virtuousness. Ruth is being brought into her new home and the community is acting as a judgment panel. Though she never is actually judged, she is offered a position with protection, and must adjust to her new life. There are great expectations for her, because the two women she's been compared to have "built up the house of Israel." She, in fact, is great-grandmother to David, the second king in Israel/Judah, and the young man who slew Goliath. Her divine strength is amazing.

> *Then all the people who were at the gate and the elders*
> *said, "We are witnesses. May the Lord make the woman,*
> *who is coming into your house, like Rachel and Leah, who*
> *together built up the house of Israel."* [52]
> ~Ruth 4:11.

When I think of the power of women working together, the story of Rachel and Leah always comes to mind. Consider Ruth's position in the Bible. Would you have been able to do what she did? Should we consider those women who are ancestors of divinities as more than human? Why/why not?

---

52. Ruth 4:11, Amplified Bible.

Practice: Create an Intention Candle

Though I think this practice is more powerful when you create a women's circle and create the candles together, you can also do this alone. Doing the practice together means your group of women can build this practice in whatever way feels good for them. Perhaps they are Christian and want to devote the ritual to Mother Mary. Maybe each person in the group worships in a different manner. Wouldn't it be nice to share a couple of words about what their intention means within their religious philosophy?

This ritual works best with a tall candle encased in glass (most grocery stores stock them, sometimes with illustrations of religious figures on them).

Think about your intention for the day, which means "what you need to work on within" (not on your to-do list). Perhaps your group could agree on a single intention? That can often be quite powerful.

Find or draw pictures of what that intention means to you and glue them to the outside of your glass candle.

As you paste the pictures or photos or drawings to your candle, say aloud what this intention means to you and what it can mean to the women around you.

When you're finished, light the candle and see how your chosen images reflect when illuminated by candlelight.

Say your intention again before blowing the candle out.

Main Takeaways from This Chapter

- Discussing the unions that created human beings
- Defining virginal mothers, wives, and sacred families
- Exploring independence and interdependence
- Thinking about female leaders in communities and cultures
- Inviting women to women

Chapter Seven
Caring for Mother Earth/Nature

When we talk about celebrating the feminine in a planetary sense, we offer Mother Earth respect and create a caring relationship that is necessary as part of our dual survival. Without caring for the world where we live, we take the chance of ruining the very earth that gives us life. It should be our first imperative to pay attention to the land that provides sustenance, and to take care of her for future generations.

Prayers to the Earth Mother or Mother Nature exist in all religions. This one is to the goddess of the Ibo people of Africa.

> *Holy Mother Earth*
> *She who guides those who live upon Her,*
> *She whose laws the people of the Ibo follow,*
> *Living in the honesty and rightness*
> *That are the ways of Goddess Ala;*
> *It is She who brings the child to the womb*
> *And She who gives it life,*
> *Always present during life*
> *And receiving those whose lives are ended,*
> *Taking them back into Her sacred womb,*
> *"the pocket of Ala."* [53]

Many women's organizations around the world exist for the purpose of protecting Mother Nature, as women have for centuries. In organizing for that purpose, these groups of women have also learned that to understand where we are now, we have to study the wealth of female wisdom of the past.

---

53. Ford, *The Hero with the African Face*, 114.

The Goddesses

Isis (Egyptian), goddess of motherhood, mourning, and healing

Gaia (Greek), personification of the earth

Aphrodite (Greek), goddess of love, beauty, and passion

Athena (Greek), goddess of war

Tiamat (Babylonian), goddess of the monstrous deep

Shekinah (Jewish), mother of fair love, fear, knowledge, and hope

White Buffalo Calf Woman (Lakota), supernatural woman and prophet

Earth Woman (Okanagan), mother of everyone

Baba Yaga (Russian), Mother Earth witch

Auset (Egyptian), goddess of crops, magic, and personal spirituality

Demeter (Greek), goddess of the grain

Artemis/Diana (Greek/Roman), goddess of wild animals and the hunt

Sequana (Gallo-Roman), goddess of ecology

Damona (Gallo-Roman), goddess of wealth and fertility

Dhat-Badan (Arabic), goddess of natural forces of the wilderness

Fatima (Arabic), moon goddess

One of the most fascinating studies of women's wisdom, especially including her knowledge of (and use of) the natural world, is Mulheres da Terra, a project that has been gathering information about women who are healers, herbalists, midwives, and shamans throughout the world. These women follow ancient traditions, carrying on the work of their foremothers, some of whom were among the earliest of the long line of divine feminine beings.

When I asked Brett Hargis about how she learned about the divine feminine, she stated: "Mother Nature or Virgin Mary? Just mentioning someone and thinking about them doesn't constitute celebration. I really feel like my life was devoid of the divine feminine when I was young. It wasn't until I got into college and contemplated paganism, Buddhism, Hinduism, and Shinto that the thought of worship outside the Holy Trinity strayed."

Before we talk about role models established by major religions, let's define eco-feminism as it relates to the divine feminine. The folks at Women and Life on Earth, an international project launched in the United States in 1999; it moved to Germany in 2001, then back to western Massachusetts in 2016, where it's currently based at the Traprock Center for Peace and Justice. WLOE defines itself as a "world-wide movement for peace through communication and translation of women's statements and actions."[54]

On WLOE's page entitled "What is ecofeminism?" there is a concise definition from Mary Mellor, author of *Feminism and Ecology*: "Ecofeminism is a movement that sees a connection between the exploitation and degradation of the natural world and the subordination and oppression of women. It emerged in the mid-1970s alongside second-wave feminism and the green movement. Ecofeminism brings together elements of the feminist and green movements, while at the same time offering a challenge to both. It takes from the green movement a concern about the impact of human activities on the non-human world and from feminism the view of humanity as gendered in ways that subordinate, exploit and oppress women."[55]

I disagree with only one thing. Some might say the ecofeminism movement began in the mid-1970s, and it may be true that the term began then,

---

54. Women and Life on Earth, http://www.wloe.org/.
55. "What Is Ecofeminism?" http://www.wloe.org/what-is-ecofeminism.76.0.html

but there has been a distinct connection between women and the world around them since the beginning of time. Though the same can be said for men, the role of Mother Nature belongs to a female. She is powerful in both destructive and compassionate ways.

Traditional Faces of Mother Earth

In a hymn written on the walls of her temple at Philae, the goddess Isis is described as the one who makes "all people live and green plants grow, who provides divine offerings to the gods," which makes her not only the Mother Earth figure, but also the one responsible for the gods' sustenance.

Other ancient civilizations that celebrated the female as creator included the Sumerians and Babylonians, who had many different names for the divine feminine and the roles goddesses played in those cultures. The flood depicted in the Bible as Noah's trials also shows up in Sumerian, Babylonian, and Hebrew mythology. According to Harvey and Baring, the floods, as depicted in Genesis, mark the end of any history or mythology about the goddess (except for the birds depicted in those early carvings).[56]

In ancient Greece, Gaia was the oldest being and the mother of all.[57] It is interesting that her power is all-encompassing, but after the Bronze Age, newer goddesses (e.g., Aphrodite, Athena, and others) are daughters of patriarchal figures like Zeus. Still, the Homeric hymns celebrate the fertility, the female's awesome powers.

Not only in Greece, but in most cultures, people tried to understand their place in the universe by worshipping a supreme being that represented them in their finest hours, as well as their worst moments. They wanted to understand both the seen and unseen, the human and the mysterious and all-powerful. The main difference between animals and human beings is that humans can create stories, a narrative of their life and the difference they might be making in their small corner of the universe.

---

56. Harvey and Baring, *The Divine Feminine.*
57. Harvey and Baring, *The Divine Feminine.*

The Greeks loved creating artistic examples of their goddesses. Think about the pastel beauty of Botticelli's Venus, the busts of powerful divinities created by anonymous sculptors who might have been slaves to the people who commissioned the busts. Homer's *Odyssey* told fantastical tales of the men and women of Greece and the gods and goddesses the people believed were in charge of the world around them.

Divine feminine beings such as Athena, said to be the manifestation of her namesake city, Athens, "the brilliant flowering of Greek civilization," is the goddess of wisdom, as well as one of the great goddesses of Greece.[58] Homer considered her important enough to the history of Greek philosophy that he physically described her as tall and beautiful, with piercing, brilliant eyes. She is physically portrayed in two different ways: one, as a helmeted warrior; the other as a proud and powerful woman in a cloak that falls from her shoulders while she holds a symbolic snake in one hand. The snake indicates her ability to rejuvenate life, which is a nod to the original goddess, Gaia. Athena receives the bard's highest nod of acceptance when she is the one who brings Odysseus home to his wife, Penelope.

Creation myths exist in all religions, but few are as chaotic as "that of the Babylonian Tiamat, goddess of the monstrous deep."[59] Tiamat (not to be confused with the five-headed dragon mother of the Dungeons and Dragons game) is the mother goddess of the salt sea, the personification of the place from which all Babylonian gods came. "She is the mother of all, and from her union with Apsu emerge all other deities."[60] If one is mother of all, that means you're the boss, right?

One of the tales about her (there aren't many) states that in a battle with Marduk (the patron god of the city of Babylon), she is killed with his arrow and ultimately split in two, creating heaven and earth with her body; the Tigris and Euphrates rivers stream from her eyes; mist is produced from her spittle; and mountains sprout from her breasts. In other words, her body is the earth upon which we live.

---

58. Harvey and Baring, *The Divine Feminine*.

59. Gyatso, "Down with the Demoness."

60. Agha-Jaffar, *Women and Goddesses in Myth and Sacred Text*, 45.

If the goddess is responsible for creating the rivers and the hills, then it is natural for other feminine beings to be responsible for its caretaking. Like one of my participants, Christina Sutcliffe, says, "I feel that any healer (male or female) is valued when they ply their craft and then often purposefully forgotten afterward—like crutches hidden in a closet, a shameful sign that there was infirmity."

In Judaism, the Shekinah (the feminine face of god) is "the intelligence within nature, the animating energy of the cosmos; rooted in tree, vine, earth, and water and active in the habitations of humanity." Though not defined as a goddess, but rather as a cosmic entity, the Shekinah is said to bring "together heaven and earth, the divine and the human in a resplendent vision of their essential relationship."[61]

The English translation says the term Shekinah means "dwelling" or "settling" and refers to that place where one might find God. Several sources refer to the Talmud's mention of the Shekinah as an actual feminine deity, while others state she is simply a voice. Whatever the case, it is obvious from the writings that she is either a feminine voice for God or one of the origin figures we see in every religion.

From passages in the Apocrypha (a collection of scriptural writings that were written between 200 BCE and 400 CE but not incorporated into the Bible), the Shekinah says,

> *I am the mother of fair love, and fear and knowledge and holy hope...*
>
> *I therefore, being eternal, am given to all my children which are named of him.*
>
> *Come unto me, all ye that be desirous of me, and fill yourselves with my fruits.*
>
> *For my memorial is sweeter than honey, and mine inheritance than the honeycomb.*[62]

---

61. Harvey and Baring, *The Divine Feminine*, 95.
62. Ecclesiasticus 24:18-20, The Bible, King James Version.

In the Native American tradition, most holy beings have some connection to the earth or animals; their female deities are powerfully linked to Mother Earth and they derive their knowledge from the world's natural healing elements.

White Buffalo Calf Woman, a Lakota supernatural woman and prophet, brought the Seven Sacred Ceremonies and the *čhaŋnúŋpa*, the sacred peace pipe, to the Lakota people. She originally appeared to some scouts as a phenomenally beautiful woman, dressed in an intricately designed white buckskin, who floated to earth from the sky.

The sacred pipe is filled with a mixture of tobacco-like products, and the strong mixture is smoked in a ceremony that includes blowing the inhaled smoke in all four directions. While packing the pipe and during the inhaling/exhaling, the smoker(s) say prayers to Mother Earth that include the admission that we are all related, that we respect the Earth and all on it, and that asks for blessings on the "two-legged" ones.[63]

From the Okanagan tribe comes the story of Earth Woman, who is the mother of everyone: "flesh is the soil; her hair is the trees and other plants. Her bones are the rocks, and her breath is the wind. She lies, her limbs and body extended, and on her body we live. When it is cold, she shivers; when it is hot, she sweats. And when she moves, there is an earthquake."[64]

When I reread that passage, it is obvious that she is the Earth, and if the Earth is "mother to everyone," we must certainly care for her, for she is powerful and filled with life force.

The story goes on to say that the Old One (who created her) also created animals and the people from pieces of Earth Woman's body. Old One says that someday everyone will be old enough to return to her and that all should "live together and revere Earth Woman as the Great Mother."[65]

---

63. Dancing to Eagle Spirit Society, "The Sacred Pipe of White Buffalo Calf Woman."

64. Leeming and Page, *Myths of the Female Divine Goddess*.

65. Leeming, *Creation Myths of the World Encyclopedia*.

The Continuing Connection to Mother Earth

The connection between Mother Earth and witchcraft is a natural one. After all, most so-called witches have an affinity for herbs and roots and are able to use them for their healing powers. My interviewee Kate Stigdon reminded me that there are other iterations of a "Mother Earth witch," such as the Russian one they call Baba Yaga. That's just one example of a culture in which Mother Earth witches are celebrated. Most Native American people have an intrinsic connection to the earth, respecting Mother Nature and recognizing that humans and nature must nurture and sustain each other for this world to survive. Similarly, other religions, philosophers, and scientists espouse the same sentiment.

In another part of the ancient world, the Egyptian goddess Auset is considered a mother goddess who, along with her husband Ausar, were the divinities Egyptians prayed to for their crops. Auset and Ausar were also known for their magic and personal spirituality. Auset's influence is beneficial in that she represents the need for good nutrition, as well as keeping clear and organic thoughts. She also reminds women that they should recognize the daily magic that happens right in front of us. The blooming of a flower in the sidewalk, the ways a hummingbird or bees can spread the fruit of the earth, the magic of a computer or a cell phone. Auset reminds us to pay close attention to everything around us and to provide care for not only our surroundings but also the people within our care.

Greek mythology gives us Demeter, goddess of the grain, who has a strong maternal instinct and extends that instinct to all manner of living things. She presides over the harvest and the earth's fertility. If you tend to be like this goddess, you may struggle to take care of yourself, because you're so busy taking care of everyone else. Anyone who is in tune with the rise and fall of the earth's seasons and who finds pleasure in seeing the first blooms come to the earth's surface shares some of Demeter's traits.

Another Greek goddess with whom eco-feminists can identify is Artemis/ Diana, goddess of wild animals and the hunt, who uses her bow and arrow to get what she wants. She's considered an environmentalist and has a great affinity for nature. Her talents are those shared by women who are most happy when they're hiking or connecting with animals in the natural world.

In the Gallo-Roman tradition, the goddess associated with ecology is the water spirit Sequana of Burgundy. Known as the goddess of the river Seine, she was said to heal all afflictions. She was named by the continental Celts, whose spirituality was animistic, meaning they believed that a spirit animated every living thing. Though Sequana is associated with the Seine River, she is also the Celtic Squan, which stands for both river and goddess. "She is mother of the clan, Snake River, bestower of health. In her arms, she carries the overflowing cornucopia of the abundant, giving land."[66]

Another Gallo-Roman goddess is Damona, whose name means "divine cow" or "great cow." She is the goddess of wealth and fertility, and there is said to be a link between curing, fertility, and regeneration. "The mother-goddesses themselves … appear at thermal spring-sanctuaries, presumably as healers themselves. There is a natural link between the mother, childbirth, and women's health before, during and after pregnancy."[67]

In the Arabian world, several goddesses represent nature in some form. Dhat-Badan, the primary goddess of the Arabs of Yemen, was a goddess of the natural forces of the wilderness, worshipped especially in tree-circled oases. She rules over the wet season in that part of the world, and people associate her with agriculture and fertility. Goatherders especially love this goddess and believe she might be responsible for dreams.

Fatima was the moon goddess in pre-Islamic Arabia. Her name means "the Creatress." She was also known as Source of the Sun, Tree of Paradise, the Moon, and Fate. She has existed from the beginning of the material world. (Not to be confused with the Our Lady of Fatima, associated with the Catholic religion.)

---

66. Quarrie, "Sequana and Blessed Water."
67. Green, *Celtic Goddesses*, 37.

Mother Nature vs. Manmade

The first use of the term man-made was in 1615,[68] and whenever I think of something that's man-made, I envision something solid and perhaps a bit cold. Buildings that constitute neighborhoods and cities are man-made, and that word is perfect to describe them. They are straight and upright, strong enough to withstand weather, masculine, and sometimes a bit austere. On the other hand, anything made by Mother Nature ("female-made" is my term for it) is colorful, soft, and natural. Hills, meadows, forests, mountains, and oceans are rounded and silent or uncontrolled and powerful, and given to rejuvenation with each coming spring. They defy anything man-made and can rip apart the man-made buildings and other "things" in mere moments.

Rachel Carson, author of *The Silent Spring* (a book that changed my life, as well as countless others'), said, "Nature has introduced great variety into the landscape, but man has displayed a passion for simplifying it. Thus, he undoes the built-in checks and balances by which nature holds the species within bounds."[69]

Carson is someone whom I call both an evolved being and a divine feminine. The reason I say that is because she changed the world by pointing out how to care for the lands and waters around us. She linked the caretaking aspect of the divine feminine with scientific evidence in order to make an argument that holds water even today, fifty years later. Without her knowledge and contributions to our body of education about the world around us, the act of simple environmentalism might have stopped with Thoreau. Instead, she shined a spotlight on what human beings had begun doing to the oceans, the rivers, the lakes, and all the other bodies of water with a commonly used insect repellent known as DDT; because of her book, even the average citizen learned how dangerous the indiscriminate use of pesticides has been to our land, as well as to ourselves. She proved that plants, birds, animals, and humans had

---

68. Merriam-Webster Dictionary, "Man-Made," https://www.merriam-webster.com /dictionary/man-made.

69. Carson, *Silent Spring*.

been harmed in some way by pesticides, and caused a revolution in the way we treated our environment.

Diane Ackerman, a multi-award-winning writer, has produced some of this century's finest close examinations of nature. She is what both her fans and critics may call a "conscientious objector" to the damage being done to our planet. A poet with more than two dozen collections to her credit, Ackerman has been praising the pastoral and writing about nature-related subjects for audiences of the *New Yorker*, *National Geographic*, and the *New York Times*. She's even been elected to the American Academy of Arts and Sciences.

She embodies traits of several of the goddesses mentioned in this book, though I'm sure she'd eschew that comparison. Ackerman has contributed to an august body of work about the mysteries surrounding us. She travels to the places about which she writes, giving an immediacy to her work that reminds us of the feminine sensitives in how we observe everything.

In fact, her book *The Rarest of the Rare* sounds a call to all naturalists or wanna-be-naturalists: "Sleepers like me need at some point to rise and take their turn on morning watch for the sake of the planet, but also for their own sake, for the enrichment of their lives. From the deserts of Namibia to the razor-backed Himalayas, there are wonderful creatures that have roamed the Earth much longer than we, creatures that not only are worthy of our respect but could teach us about ourselves."[70]

Does that call draw you, entice you to take action? Ackerman's words call for all of us—divine or otherwise, male or female-oriented—to care for the Mother Earth represented in so many ways in our various theologies.

In 2004, Wangari Maathai, founder of the Green Belt Movement, was born in Kenya, but educated in the United States and Germany before returning to Nairobi for her PhD. The first woman in East and Central Africa to receive a PhD, she became chair of the Veterinary Anatomy department at the University of Nairobi, her alma mater.

---

70. Ackerman, *The Rarest of the Rare*.

Maathai first introduced the idea of community-based tree planting in 1976, then built on that idea and broadened it to become the Green Belt Movement. By simply planting trees, she made inroads into reducing poverty and conserving the environment in the communities which chose to participate. Her grassroots organizing gained momentum and ultimately Maathai became a world-recognized expert in environmentalism and human rights, and was named a UN Messenger of Peace. As a result of her work, African nations like her native Kenya began recognizing the need to safeguard their public lands and to practice conservation techniques like those she and her widening sphere of environmental trusts recommend.[71]

Like Maathai, Winona LaDuke is a leader both in environmentalism and political activism. She lives and works on the White Earth reservation in northern Minnesota. Her focus issues are sustainable renewable energy and food systems, and she speaks regularly on those topics to groups as large and influential as the United Nations, and as impactful as the International Council of Indigenous Women. She ran for the office of vice president alongside presidential hopeful Ralph Nader on two occasions.

LaDuke is founder of the White Earth Land Recovery Project, and in that role, she works within the White Earth community to protect the land and to keep native plants. But she has gone far beyond her local community and brings her considerable knowledge to the rest of the world via her role as Program Director for Honor the Earth.

In her TED talk, LaDuke says that food "comes from our relatives," whether our relatives have hooves, fins, wings, or two legs. She refers to her Ojibwe roots and the story of how the creator told her people to move to the place where they are and to make wild rice, that it would sustain them. She points to other civilizations and their own relationship to food. Each of the stories she tells includes a bit of the creation story of that civilization, and how that creation story is related to the foods native to each. She points out the problems with genetic engineering and how many food plants have become extinct—the food ancestors are disappearing. She lists the number of dietary illnesses that are the result of loss of access to our traditional foods.

71. The Green Belt Movement, http://www.greenbeltmovement.org/.

She talks about how seven corporations have ownership over a great number of seeds available to the world.[72]

LaDuke, like the other women mentioned, points to the small community, the family community, and relates how what happens to that community affects the larger, global community. We can look at this as the contemporary embodiment of the female creators. She can be likened to one of the divine feminine charged with caring for the world.

If you plant ancient varieties of tomatoes or if you're interested in bringing bees back to your garden, in your own way, you're doing the same kind of work as Winona LaDuke and her White Earth Land Project.

In South America, a woman named Berta Isabel Cáceres Flores recognized that the Agua Zarca Dam being built on the Gualcarque River would irrevocably damage the lives of the Lenca people, because the dam's construction would cut off water, medicine, and food for hundreds of the Lenca (by the way, they owned the land and weren't consulted about the dam, which was an international violation of indigenous people's rights).

Cáceres, a Lenca herself, was raised by a strong mother who encouraged her daughter to stand up for her rights, a lesson Cáceres learned well. She became a student activist and started the National Council of the Popular and Indigenous Organizations of Honduras in 1993, when she was in her late teens. She fought against illegal logging, battling large organizations though her life, as well as her colleagues' lives, was continually threatened. In 2016, this well-known environmentalist and activist lost her battle when she was murdered in her own home.[73]

When caring for the earth, as well as for the soul, it is important that everyone recognizes the need and attends to it. People of all genders must exert their divine feminine connections to the world around them in order to heal the wounds we've afflicted. Laura Hosford, creator of the Light Leaders Academy, states, "As we begin to open our hearts, minds and souls to align

72. Honor the Earth, "Winona LaDuke."
73. Treesisters, "Berta Isabel Cáceres Flores."

with these beautiful divine feminine energies once again on the Earth we can begin to embrace more of our own Divine qualities of unconditional love, compassion, grace, beauty, intuition, flow, abundance, joy, creative genius, collaboration, integrity, respect, patience and nurturance bringing us into a state of wholeness and inner balance."

A group of women in California called "The Sisters of the Valley" grow and harvest their own cannabis and hearken back to pre-Christian practices. They create balms and ointments made from the cannabis they grow, with a goal of improving their clients' physical and emotional health. The group specifically focuses on freeing women by entering into a "commercial relationship and earning a wage or commission," says one of their leaders, Sister Kate. The group has taken on a nun persona, though they are not in any way associated with the Catholic religion.

This group is harvesting an herb that has long been known for its medicinal qualities, as well as its ability to morph itself into usable materials. Now that more states are recognizing the healing elements of cannabis-based products, it feels like a natural move for these women to take on the roles their foremothers did back when they would have been called witches.

A few years ago, I joined an international online class to read books about historical fiction about plagues, witches, and war. I thought the reading list was fascinating, but I didn't realize how eye-opening it would be until we began reading *The Physick Book of Deliverance Dane* by Katherine Howe.

Having grown up in New England, I knew the story of the Salem witches very well. It's a story that goes from the present back to the days when our country was new, a time when religious beliefs leaned toward a fervor that I find hard to explain. The fear of God caused people to commit crimes that can only be described as insane.

Communities placed women they believed to be witches in stocks in the middle of the town square, forcing those women to forget whatever talents they might have as healers and terrifying them so much that they would completely abandon their own abilities. Women were hanged, sometimes burned at the stake, and often simply run out of town or killed quietly in their own homes.

The women who carry on as "Salem witches" today bank on the curiosity of visitors to Salem, often acting as somewhat of a sideshow; however, they also carry on a tradition of good works, as espoused by Laurie Cabot, the Witch of Salem. In the 1990s, Massachusetts' Governor Michael Dukakis recognized Cabot with the Patriot Award, given to her because of her special work with children and people with special needs.

In the class, we discussed the treatment of women and how the men in the stories appeared threatened by the special talents the women had (of Howe's story, as well as others we read in the class). We talked about the magic of women being more of an internal type of wisdom, an ability to reflect and collaborate, a softer and more receptive way of dealing with those around them. Yes, the women had a talent with herbs or tinctures, but without their ability to listen to the people who came to them, their healing powers would have been thwarted.

My Story: What the Ancestors Know

I've always had a special affinity for gardens, beginning with the days at my grandmother's house where she taught me the names of the dainty and pungent flowers that lined her driveway, as well as teaching me about the weeds that would try to squeeze out the English cottage garden flowers. I lived in the projects, a place where small patches of weeds were bordered by large swaths of concrete, so a garden was a magical thing for me, and every time I visited her, I marveled at the birds and butterflies that visited her house but never came to mine.

Years later, I'd have my own apartment, and I began experimenting with window boxes, hanging spider plants and Swedish ivy in every window. If I couldn't have dirt to dig in, I brought it inside. I grew basil and oregano, aloe and lavender, and eventually, I had a house with an acre of land, and I planted that with vegetables. Lots of vegetables.

If I lean back in my chair right now, I can smell the spring earth after we'd turned the bed. I can feel the grit of the dirt under my fingertips, and I can taste that fresh squirt of the first tomato of the season. Even though my back ached for days after we prepared the soil for that first garden (and I harvested more rocks than vegetables), I'd never felt closer to my grandmother, though she had long since passed. All those lessons she taught me when I was a girl wandering through the lilies, nasturtiums, and bluebells of her backyard garden came back as though she stood next to me, whispering in my ear, "Never chase away the bees. They're our friends, but these guys, these slugs…they need to be removed." She'd pluck them with the fingertips of her rubber gloves, and plop, they'd go into a can of my grandfather's beer.

Other women taught me about gardening after those first lessons with my grandmother. When I lived in a small ranch house in upstate New York, my next-door neighbor taught me the value of planting marigolds next to tomatoes to keep away our woodland friends who wanted to snack before I could. In Vermont, my friend Chris showed me how to pinch back new growth so that plants would produce more and larger vegetables. The women I knew would talk about our gardens when we went out for a drink after working all day at the local restaurants. I learned about the mushrooms to avoid and the tricks to keep deer away. I discovered that a group of herbs and natural flowers rolled together creates a magical sense of peace. I enjoyed the aural pleasures of a field of lavender from a woman who specialized in Oriental massage. My friends would make me a peppermint tea when my stomach acted up, and they'd offer a tincture of ginger for my annual winter cough. All my teachers were women.

I didn't realize what an ancient group I'd been admitted into, but I knew that it felt right and natural to sit and listen to my body and to treat it with herbal remedies rather than pills.

I thought of my grandmother and her ability to see a flower that needed to be hand-pollinated, and I thought of my girlfriends who had shown me the ancient lessons of planting at the right time of the moon, and I thought of the abilities all these women had to heal those they loved (as well as some they didn't). It struck me that these stories were far more influential than anything I'd ever learned, for these women were teaching me how to live according to the land.

Reflection

Daughter RavynStar wrote the *Journeying into the Goddess* blog that mentions Julunguul. Julunggul is the Aborigine goddess associated with fertile rains and seas and is considered a rainbow serpent and also sees the maturation process of boys to men. She's unique in her role with boys and men, since most goddesses either relate directly to all of humankind or to women. In this quote, she encourages a connection with those symbolic rains:

> *If it rains today, it is a sign of Julunggul's blessing.*
> *Release your inner child and dance in the downpour.*
> *Jump in puddles and let Her fertile, productive energy*
> *splash freely all over your life and everything around you.*[74]
> ~Daughter RavynStar

I love this quote because it encourages us to enjoy being innocent and childlike. Every day, we learn more about the environment. Think about how women are connected with the earth as you consider this quote. What do you do when you feel most free? Do it now. Then write about it.

Practice: The Nest

I have a ritual. Every night when the sun goes down, I close the blinds on every window in my house. I do it deliberately, slowly, mindfully. I gaze out each window, checking the neighborhood, noting which lights are on, how the sunlight/moonlight looks as it illuminates the tall pine trees in the island dominating our little cul-de-sac. Then I light a few candles in front of my fireplace and, if it's wintertime, I light the fire. Room by room, I turn on the small stained- glass lamps that I love because they bring a warmth to the closed-in spaces. I think about the good that has come from my day, the little challenges I won—perhaps meeting a page limit I'd set or getting all of my errands done or making time to cook a pot of New England fish chowder.

---

74. Daughter RavynStar, "Journeying into the Goddess."

Call it a moment of gratitude or whatever you like, but that ritual keeps me grounded and reminds me that no matter what goes wrong, there'll be an equal number of things that have gone right.

I've envied some of the women who nest so well that I long to visit their homes just to sink into their velvet armchairs and sip from their rose-colored porcelain teacups. I remember one of my girlfriends had a habit of throwing a flimsy scarf over the lamps wherever she went. I swear she kept dozens of them in her purse. That simple toss of material was her way of nesting. She made each space her own by covering the ugly lamp with a diffuser, a scarf that filtered out the ugly and created a sensuality—much like the one she wore in the arch of her eyebrow and the crooked way she smiled.

As guardians of the home-fire, I can imagine some of the paintings on cave walls may have been created by the women who simply needed something other than a blank wall to look at. It's possible that other early artists created the story of their family on those walls or created images relating to a traumatic event that happened to the community. Perhaps some of those household cave walls held images of her children. We may never know the truth of who the cave artists were or their specific intentions, but I imagine the divine feminine images on those walls.

Candles, aromatherapy, herbal teas, soothing creams, and remedies for everything from lovesickness to a toothache. Today, most of those ingredients are found in almost all of my female friends' homes. Everywhere. But many women throughout history have died for keeping the same ingredients in their own homes.

Every culture has tales of the women who know just which bark makes the tea that takes away a horrible headache, or who can grow an herbal garden of scented plants designed to spark creativity or to entice the love you want in your life. Long before men became the leaders in the medical field, medicine women held a revered place in the community as the ones who healed both physical and psychological ills. It was a natural and accepted way of life.

Then for various (and sometimes unknown) reasons, the women became suspected of talents too powerful for normal human beings. Whether the woman mixed her herbs in old England, on the Saharan desert, or in a small village in China, she became the target of scorn and ridicule. Few understood her talents nor cared enough to learn what she knew about plants, living organisms, and the secrets of recognizing the elements of the natural world that were helpful, as well as those that were not. Instead, most people overlooked the benefit of a woman's botanical and natural knowledge.

Main Takeaways from this Chapter

- Analyzing how different cultures see Mother Nature
- Introducing ecofeminist role models
- Discussing the feminine affinity for healing
- Exploring natural vs. manmade

The Goddesses

Inanna/Ishtar (Egyptian/Babylonian), goddess of sensuality and warfare, as well as the goddess for animals and everything that grows

Grandmother Woodchuck (Abenaki), wise old woman who raises a hero

Deer Woman (Plains), associated with love and fertility

Spider Woman (Navajo), taught humans to weave

Fox Woman (Cree/Ojibwe), wise elder spirit

Diana/Artemis (Roman/Greek), goddess of the hunt and domesticated animals, and also acts as the moon goddess and protector of newborns

Ninhursag (Sumerian), goddess of wild and herd animals

Nerrivik (Eskimo), goddess who rules over sea creatures

Chapter Eight

Connecting with Animals

I've loved a number of animals in my lifetime—mostly cats and dogs, but some birds and fish, and maybe even a turtle or two—and most all of the women I know also have a soft spot for animals, even though they might never have them in their homes. My interviewee, Melissa Seligman, states that she "feels connected to a lot of animals. But horses draw me in more than anything else." I never really thought much of it, because I took it for granted that we just love our pets, but the connection we have with animals taps into our ability to be caretakers. Many women have made inroads by researching and caring for animals, such as elephants, chimpanzees, gorillas, orangutans, and dogs: Jane Goodall (chimpanzees), Dame Daphne Sheldrick (African elephants), Dian Fossey (gorillas), Birute Galdikas (orangutans), Lek Chailert (Asian elephants), Jill Robinson (black bears), and many other women who've pulled back the curtain on the suffering of animals at the hands of large corporations and a patriarchal society.

The female of our human species is as protective of animals as the females of the animal species are protective of their own. According to Emily Garder, author of *Women and the Animal Rights Movement*, 80 percent of the members of the movement are female.[75] As she rightly points out, that can be both a deterrent and a false-positive, because women do not necessarily join the movement solely because of emotion, but for the reason that being part of the movement gives them the ability to be a change-maker.

If you study the work being done to save certain animal species, as well as to learn more about others, you'll discover that a lot of the important work is headed by women (we'll talk about them more specifically later in this chapter). And as I stated in my intro, the divine feminine traits aren't embodied strictly

---

75. Garder, *Women and the Animal Rights Movement*.

by those who identify as female; a lot of the people who identify as male also work with animals and embody those caretaking, intuitive, and reflective traits necessary to watch, listen, and learn about the animal world around us. However, as Garder points out, women are more likely to become activists because of their nature to have a "greater affinity or compassion for animals."

The Vegan Feminist Network, founded by scholar Corey Wrenn, states that their "mission is to non-violently eradicate oppression from the Nonhuman Animal rights movement and improve inclusiveness through dialogue and education."[76] Vegetarian feminists are concerned that the oppression and killing of animals for human consumption is parallel to the oppression of women in a patriarchal society. As in ecofeminism, there's a strong connection between the domination of women and the domination of nature. If we respect all living beings and fight against their oppression, the vegetarian feminist movement posits, then we can create a more peaceful existence.

Whether you're a vegetarian feminist, an activist for the humane treatment of animals, a lover of dolphins, or simply a responsible pet owner, the attributes you embody are similar to those that shaped our early perceptions of the feminine deities who created strong bonds with the animal world.

Animal Partners

Many depictions of goddesses and other divine feminine beings in the world's theologies show the divinity with an animal. Though the animal might be a metaphor for the attribute the deities are known for (i.e., a deer is swift-footed, as was the goddess Diana), their very presence next to the divine feminine suggests a connection between the goddess and the animal. When one sees a male god with an animal, it is often engaged with the animal in a combative state, but with the female deities, the depiction is usually benign.

Carvings and statues of Inanna-Ishtar (ca. 2300-2000 BCE) show a female figure, with the wings and taloned feet of a bird, standing on the backs of two lions. A complex goddess, Inanna-Ishtar is the goddess of sensuality, yet also

76. Wrenn, Vegan Feminist Network.

a goddess of warfare, as noted in earlier chapters; however, her representation as a bird-animal cements the metaphor of her abilities, equaling the power of a lion with the lion of the sky. She is one of the few feminine deities whose connection with animals is similar to that of the masculine. The odd juxtaposition of her sensuality vs. her ability to command war creates a sort of balance of feminine and masculine attributes, sensuality normally being the domain of the feminine, while warfare is normally conducted by patriarchal societies.

In many Native American legends, a woman either gives birth to the world or is the first inhabitant. The Iroquois speak about the woman who dreams about land before it exists, and when she is pushed from the Great Blue to the world below, she is aided in her fall by a Fish Hawk, who provides her a soft landing onto the back of a great turtle. She gives birth to a daughter who then spawns the rest of the human race.

That very first connection during the birth of the world between the mother and animals is indicative of how much respect the Native American culture gives to those beings who share the earth with us. Throughout the many stories told by storytellers from the hundreds of Native American tribes, animals reign as major characters.

Among the animal spirits/deities recognized by various tribes, a number are female and represent important stories told by native peoples. In the Abenaki tradition, stories are told of Grandmother Woodchuck, the wise old female who raised Glooskap, the Wabanaki hero. The Woodlands and Central Plains tribes tell tales of Deer Woman, a spirit associated with love and fertility. Spider Woman, an important deity in the Navajo nation, taught humans how to weave, and Fox Woman plays a wise elder spirit in the Cree and Ojibwe tribes.

Diana (Roman)/Artemis (Greek) are two halves of the same goddess, who is often depicted with a deer or large hound at her side. Said to be the goddess of the hunt, few realize that she's also known as the goddess of domesticated animals. Since she is always shown with a bow and arrow in her hands, we can assume that she would hunt the deer with the dog at her side.

Ninhursag, a goddess of the Sumerian people, is said to be the mother of both the wild and the herd animals. Her temple was marked with a sacred herd of cattle, which makes it logical that she is called the Great Cow, because her milk nourishes all life on earth as well as the Sumerian people.

Around the same time in world history, Ishtar, the Green One or She of the Springing Verdure, was the Babylonian goddess for animals and everything that grows. A temple gate constructed in her honor, made of a deep-blue lapis lazuli, was adorned with goldish-brown reliefs of aurochs, the animals that were the predecessors for cattle. The gate and the walkway leading from it (the processional way) were used once a year for a harvest festival. The event lasted twelve days, beginning right after the vernal equinox. Ishtar is also worshipped as the Mistress of Heaven and is believed to be the symbol of sexual energy/fertility.

Artemis, the moon goddess, descends from the Neolithic goddess of the animals, and those who worship her have practiced rites and dances in Turkey for thousands of years. She has been called many names (as so many goddesses are), but the one she's connected with most frequently is Cybele. As she derives her power from the Great Goddess, Artemis is known for the ability to both generate life and to destroy it. In Greece, where people worshipped her more than other goddesses, she was known to guard any newborns, whether human or animal.

In Eskimo folk tales, Nerrivik is a goddess who rules over the sea creatures. When the hunters cannot find seal to catch, they ask her for help, and she sends seals to them if the men/wizards help her comb her hair (she only has one hand, because she was punished for leaving her husband and running away with her brothers. Her grandfather cut off Nerrivik's hands when she tried to cling to the side of the boat after she was blamed for causing a great storm).

All of the goddesses mentioned, particularly those directly related to animals or posing as such, are "wilder" than the others we've already mentioned. They are inclined to be fighters, as their female counterparts in the animal world are. They will protect their charges with their lives, and they're not beings that stand for trifling. If you are likely to rescue baby squirrels or to derive great pleasure from the sight of a wild animal, or your dream is to build an animal shelter or to become actively involved in preventing an animal's extinction, your divine feminine qualities are derived from these early feminine deities responsible for caring for the animal kingdom.

Contemporary Animal Goddesses

Many of the women working with animals today battle some of the worst conditions, spending years trying to accustom dangerous animals to a human presence, yet they continue to do so. In fact, 90 percent of the world's primate sanctuaries are run by women.[77] Louis Leakey, an anthropologist based in Kenya, was responsible for hiring three of the most celebrated female primatologists, women who ultimately changed the way we look at primates today.

Jane Goodall, Dian Fossey, and Birute Galdikas, all women without experience working with primates, were hired by Leakey not for their talents but because of their abilities to pick up on non-verbal cues. "[W]omen were inherently patient and silent observers, whereas men were ambitious hierarchical careerists. A life of near-poverty watching animals live out long lives for ten hours a day, decade by decade, was not going to turn men on at all."[78]

Goodall, who works with chimpanzees in Gombe, Africa, stunned the scientific world with her studies of chimps. Instead of conducting her research academically, the way male primatologists did, when twenty-six-year-old Jane began studying her chimps in 1960, she named them. But that's not what shocked the scientific world. It was the ability to sit with her subjects for days that enabled Goodall to see the roles the chimps played in their environment, to identify the emotional bonds they had with each other, and to recognize their kinship with human beings.

For the past fifty years, she has brought her research to both paleontologists and the world, as a whole, and even in her mid-eighties, she continues the fight she began so long ago. Millions of people around the world have learned

---

77. Jahme, *Beauty and the Beasts.*
78. Jahme, *Beauty and the Beasts.*

about endangered species and have joined in protecting them because of Dr. Goodall's writings and public appearances.

Another of Leakey's hires, Dian Fossey lost her life in 1985 after fighting to save the mountain gorilla in Rwanda. Fossey cultivated an interest in primates when she visited Leakey in Tanzania at the Olduvai Gorge in 1963, three years after Goodall started her work with chimps. But it was a visit to Travellers Rest, a small hotel in Uganda, and a trek in to see the mountain gorillas with Walter Baumgartel, that convinced Fossey she would be back to study the gorillas. A few years later, Fossey and Leakey met again, and this time, she showed him the articles she'd published about Africa. He knew she was committed, had a deep love for animals, and had worked with children—all necessary components for someone who would spend extensive amounts of time patiently watching and documenting animal behavior. He hired her, and soon she was off to the Congo to begin work.

Like Goodall before her, Dian Fossey mimicked the animals she studied, worked hard to get them comfortable in her presence, and fought equally hard to bring their story to the public. She found the shy gorillas to be protective of their children and their family units, but after habituating them to her daily visits, they accepted her into the fold. Unlike Goodall, Fossey often ruffled feathers in the community, as well as with the politicos where she tirelessly worked to protect the gorillas from poaching.

The third in Leakey's triumvirate of primate women is Birute Galdikas, a Lithuanian-Canadian who has become the world's most knowledgeable primatologist specializing in orangutans. Galdikas' work with orangutans in Borneo began after she convinced Leakey in 1969 (when she was a grad student at UCLA) to help her find the funding to study orangutans, in spite of being warned that the jungle setting where the primates lived and their notorious shyness would make research impossible. She proved everyone wrong, setting up Camp Leakey, maintaining her research, and delivering the *National Geographic* cover story on her findings four years later.

Like Fossey and Goodall, Galdikas found a social structure among orangutans, observed the animals, and documented their eating and mating habits.

And like her colleague, Jane Goodall, Birute Galdikas has devoted her life to her research. After forty years in Tanjung Puting, now a national park, Galdikas has the honor of being the person who has conducted the longest continuous study of any of the world's wild mammals.[79]

Many other women possess the divine feminine ability to work with animals and to contribute to the research about them as Goodall, Fossey, and Galdikas have. Lek Chailert in Thailand and Dame Daphne Sheldrick in Kenya have both contributed to saving the lives of abused and endangered elephants. Chailert works with her husband at her camp, Save Elephant Foundation, in Chiang Mai, Thailand, saving not only Asian elephants but any other abused or abandoned animal she discovers. Joy Adamson, the author of *Born Free*—the story about raising a lion cub with her husband—dedicated her life to studying lions, as well as to raising money to protect wildlife. In the marine world, Margaret Howe Lovatt is known for her work with dolphins. Her project, funded by NASA, helped her study a dolphin named Peter, and to teach him rudimentary language skills. Biologist Diane Boyd has spent the last fourteen years studying wolves in her post as large carnivore specialist in Montana. She studies the wolves' family groups, how the animals travel, and how they deal with conflicts.

It's my guess that this is the tip of an iceberg that could fill an entire set of encyclopedias.

If you find that your talent is the neighborhood equivalent of being an animal whisperer, you embody some of the same determination as the goddess Diana or Dian Fossey, the wisdom of the Plains Indian's Deer Woman or Birute Galdikas. Your commitment to saving the whales or protecting the condor is divine. Your love for the broad-billed hummingbird that comes to your garden every summer lifts your spirit during that brief human-animal connection before the bird flits away. If you love the beings that share the world with us, I would call that divine.

---

79. Orangutan.org, "Biography, Dr. Birute Mary Galdikas."

My Story: The Female Mahout

In 2015, I traveled through Thailand, stopping to visit an elephant sanctuary in the center of the country near the River Kwai, the river made famous in the World War II-era movie of the same name. I was with a group of more than twenty Americans as we toured Bangkok, Ayutthaya, and Kanchanaburi. After a week of traveling with our rather interesting group, I took off by myself in the long cigarette boat that ferried us to and from the jungle resort on the river where we were staying.

Nothing is more exotic than speeding between jungle-covered cliffs in a twenty-foot-long boat just wide enough to seat two people side by side, but long enough for half a dozen. The air, heavy with the previous evening's downpour, moved like liquor through my nostrils. Though the wind rushing by should have cooled me, I still had to pull my shirt from my back when I transferred from the boat to a little red truck waiting for me on the dock.

An hour and a half later, the truck wheezed onto a tiny dirt road that wound past craters and around trees before finally coming to a stop at a large cement building that was built about twelve feet off the ground. If I looked toward the mountains surrounding us, I could see the heads of the elephants I'd come to work with for the day.

That morning, all I was concerned about was connecting with the huge grey beasts that my mother had loved her whole life. I was there to pay homage to her, but I didn't realize that I'd fall in love with her animals as she had.

I remember almost every moment of that experience. I can describe each of the elephants, as well as the volunteers who helped us make the calcium balls we fed the older bulls. I didn't think I'd ever be able to wash off the mud and pieces of vegetables and fruits that covered my hands. But the one moment that was more magical than all the rest happened early that morning, when I was one of only a few people on the platform where the elephants were being fed their breakfast.

The light in that part of Thailand is almost a golden-green, especially in the morning, and it creates a type of magic that makes everything seem like it's moving in slow motion. Through that light, I heard the sound of singing. I couldn't understand the words, nor did I know the music, but the singing came from where the elephants had gathered. A Thai song, I thought.

I moved closer to the end of the platform where the mahouts stood talking and laughing. Each elephant had one who handled him/her.

Below the platform, a tall woman dressed all in black stood next to an old, blind, female elephant. The Japanese woman had once been a stockbroker who earned enough money to be considered rich by anyone's standards. At some point during one of her vacations, she came to the sanctuary and met the elephant she now serenaded with her lullaby. She never left, though she faced the reality that being a mahout is a career normally reserved for Thai men. I thought about that as I watched the elephant lean its head against the woman's back as though following the sound as it rumbled through the woman's body.

The stockbroker had gone back to work but something about that elephant called to her, and ultimately, she gave up her life to come to the sanctuary to learn how to be a mahout for this big, blind old girl. Though the woman is only in charge of the welfare of one elephant and will probably never make the inroads that activists like Lek Chailert (who runs a sanctuary in Chiang Mai and speaks internationally about animal welfare), this Japanese woman exhibited more divine feminine qualities in the short time I observed her than almost everyone I've ever met.

Reflection

Kris Waldherr, the award-winning author and illustrator of adult and children's books, writes about goddesses in her latest book, released by Touchstone Books in 2019. This quote came from her book *Doomed Queens*. Though Waldherr talks about another Diana in this quote (Princess Diana of England), the connection between Princess Diana and the goddess Diana is clear.

> *At her funeral, Diana's brother observed, "Of all the*
> *ironies about Diana, perhaps the greatest was this—a girl*

given the name of the ancient goddess of hunting was, in
the end, the most hunted person of our modern age."[80]

~ Charles Spencer, Ninth Earl Spencer, as quoted by
Kris Waldherr

Diana, the goddess of the hunt, is connected with wild animals and the moon.

Imagine her howling with the wolves or running through the woods with her arrow ready to fly. Her athleticism aligns her more with the animal kingdom than with humans, yet her hunting skills are famed, and the goddess never appears to be vulnerable. Diana is one of the strongest young female goddesses.

Perhaps you can consider whether the contemporary women who work with animals embody some of the same personality aspects as the goddesses who have animal familiars, as you respond to this quote about Princess Diana and her connection to her namesake goddess.

Which traits of hers do you embody? You don't have to be a runner or an archer to be a goddess of the hunt.

Practice: Face to Face, Even Virtually

One of the many things that animals teach us is that they have rituals. Certain birds have mating dances: domesticated dogs practice the ritual of turning round and round and round before settling down (even though they no longer have to tamp down the ground, as they did when they were wild), and many wild animals express their grief for mates' or family members' deaths in rituals that may mimic the ones we practice.

The most important ritual I believe we all should practice is meeting face to face and expressing our pleasure for seeing those we love. During the pandemic, this was a ritual that we all missed, because as humans we need that physical touch; we need to see a person's face, to hug them, or to simply offer

---

80. Charles Spencer, full text of oration at Princess Diana's funeral.

a handshake. I am sure that therapists worldwide recorded an overload of humans who became depressed as a result of the lack of physical contact.

Even if you might be unable to meet with your loved ones for a much-needed hug, you can still practice that ritual by wrapping your arms around yourself, and breathe deeply and quietly, for a few moments each day. If you have a dog or cat, sit with them while stroking their fur, silently and intently, for five minutes. Not only will you receive a dose of the feel-good hormone, oxytocin, but your blood pressure and heart rate will stabilize or lower. (And your pet feels that contentment, as well).

Main Takeaways from This Chapter

- Considering the power of women to connect with animals
- Examining the goddesses and their animal partners
- Studying contemporary women changing the animal world

The Goddesses

Marguerite Porete (French), one of the Beguine (holy women) of the thirteenth century

Durga (Hindu), the mother-protector

Judith (Hebrew), warrior and pious widow

Athena (Greek), goddess of education

Chapter Nine

Dreams and Careers

Dolores Carr, one of my interviewees, summed up our roles in American culture succinctly: "Our American culture has been run by men, for the most part. I believe that if nurturing women continued in taking up fundamental roles in society, it could bring a working structure, a meaningful action, and perhaps even peace to corrupt and oftentimes greedy actions of the men in power."

If all of society recognized the divine feminine, it would mean that all voices of feminine wisdom and contributions as caregivers would be valued in the home, community, and workplace. If that's the case, then those who raise the family and keep the home would be as highly valued as those who run corporations.

One of the attributes that determines our dreams and careers is the ability to teach. It's always been true that most teachers are women. All mothers are women; therefore, all mothers teach, even those who are dysfunctional or absent. In fact, that passive kind of teaching is often more impactful, leaving children confused by the lack of mothering in their lives. Our mothers are our first teachers, yet for the rest of our lives, we are likely to be managed or supervised by men in almost every aspect of our lives, even our deepest, most personal lives: our spiritual lives. When I talk to women about the first pieces of feminine wisdom they remember, they invariably say it came from their mothers or grandmothers—the women who taught them how to say their first words, how to walk, how to read, how to care for others, how to find their way home. The women are the first teachers, the first leaders, the caregivers.

However, in no place is there more disparity between the feminine and the masculine than in religion. With very few exceptions throughout the world, the masculine role is dominant. The leaders are predominantly male (or imagined to be male because of the god's characteristics), and often, women are dissuaded from adding their voice to religious writings. For example, Marguerite Porete, a holy woman who was part of the thirteenth-century Beguine movement, wrote a spiritual treatise called *The Mirror of Simple Souls*. She believed that love and God were one and the same, but when she wrote about her spiritual process and the work became popular, the church put her on trial, ultimately burning her at the stake. That's enough to quiet a whole generation of women. It takes immense bravery and courage to speak out, even when you're teaching about love. When you're feeling like you need that strength, think of the many goddesses and holy women who came before you, and plumb the courage they had, because you have that same bravery inside of your heart.

To be honest, I don't remember who I'd say was the first to teach me about God in heaven. The process felt almost sponge-like for me, deriving a bit of information from my parents and grandparents, but also from church and school. But I am not you, and your experience is likely very different. We all have our own stories. Maybe my mother taught me my prayers. It could have been my grandmother. Every night, I sang a little off-key chorus as we knelt before the bed: "Now I lay me down to sleep, I pray the Lord my soul to keep. If I should die before I wake, I pray the Lord my soul to take." I hear that prayer now, and it sounds so fearful, and I know why. Created as a blessing passed from mothers to their children during times of plague and disease and the sudden nighttime deaths of little ones, it was the mother's way of placing one last blessing over her most precious ones, in the hope that if one of her children were to die, entrance to heaven would be paved. Perhaps the woman who initially taught her child this prayer had already lost children and wanted to serve the plea for this child's safety directly to the Lord. Perhaps that woman thought God would listen more quickly to a child than to its parents. Perhaps this was an appeal for protection.

How powerful are the first lessons in a human being's spiritual understanding of the world around her and where she fits within it? If that early education came from a woman, if the very foundation of your culture's philosophical understanding of itself was taught by that woman, and the child's path was informed by those lessons, then why turn the second half of that child's life over to the patriarchal half of the community's leaders? Those early formative years, from the moment that baby recognizes him- or herself, through puberty, are the years when the majority of everything we believe is taught to us. Yet those early leaders have traditionally not remained our teachers, our trusted ones, our caretakers, or our role models. Instead, the leadership in the world has been structured according to a patriarchal society, mimicking the same hierarchy you see in religions: women may be nuns or abbesses or teachers, but few are in the upper echelon of religious administration (with the exception of the Baha'i faith, which encourages equality). Compare the record-breaking thirty-seven female CEOs on the Fortune 500 list (less than 8 percent of the total number) to the smaller number of women in religious leadership addressed in a Pew Research report, and you can see how the two relate to each other.[81]

Why am I talking about religion and Fortune 500 companies in the same sentence when this chapter is entitled Dreams and Careers? Because, for many of us, the permission to dream about the possibilities in our life came from the lessons taught by the mother. If she was beaten down, unsure of her worth, and unable to forge a way for herself because of the restrictions of society, then it's more likely that she will pass along fear to us. She will teach us to be afraid. If the mother feels deserving of respect and knows that her strengths are appreciated, she is more likely to pass that empowerment on to her child. Depending on which end of the spectrum that mother feels divine, she will share with the ones for which she cares. On the other hand, if you were raised by a strong mother or a society that supports the feminine strengths, you are more likely to succeed in tough situations like climbing the corporate ladder.

Quite a few of the women I spoke with were frustrated with their leaders. Patricia Latin said, "My religion did not have any concept of women as divine or even as leaders. Women were not allowed to teach men; they could only

---

81. *Fortune*, "Fortune 500," 2020; Sandstrom, "Women Relatively Rare in Top Positions of Religious Leadership."

teach children and other women. They were also required to be subject to men. This is one of the reasons that I left the religion at a fairly young age and currently have no interest in organized religion."

That understanding of the balance of power in our world is so ingrained in the people I've spoken to that the majority of women answering my question about whether we should celebrate the feminine or a goddess said that we should not. That surprised me, because I had hoped that women could see themselves in the same dignified manner that those very first goddesses did. Then I thought about it and, listing off the major religions of the world, I thought about the spiritual leader of each of them. It was a long time before I remembered several religions headed by women, but they are not among the major religions of the world.

It's fascinating that women—across the board, no matter their cultures, home country, philosophical beliefs—said they didn't want to celebrate the feminine. A clear 90 percent of those who answered that question, replied, "No, I have no interest in celebrating the feminine."

I wish I had asked "why?" after I'd posed that question to them, but I did not, so I add it in conversation if I'm talking face-to-face to someone about their beliefs. The subject comes up often, and again and again, I'm surprised by female reluctance to celebrate strong, holy, powerful goddesses.

Since I don't have enough data, I can't answer the question, yet it would make perfect sense if the hesitation to place a female deity on a level beside or at least close to the ultimate holy one is the result of this male-dominated society we've lived in since the farming age, about twelve thousand years ago.[82] We are used to accepting the male of any species as the stronger. That's the result of nature more than culture. So, it would be understandable if celebrating a goddess would be akin to breaking the most basic of all cultural and religious rules: totally flipping the script.

---

82. Anasathwamy and Douglas, "The Origins of Sexism."

Personal Power

Hinduism shows us more divine feminine faces than any other major religion, so let's start talking about the goddesses who are leaders, who serve and create rather than subjugate or dominate, as this section title states. Women are mentioned as being present during early academic philosophical debates; they are scholars, teachers, and gurus.

In chapter 47 of the *Anushasana Parva* (the thirteenth book of eighteen in the Indian epic *Mahabharata*, a historical retelling of two Indian families), a daughter's value is compared to a son's: "The daughter, O king, has been ordained in the scriptures to be equal to the son."[83] Yet this supposed equality doesn't exist throughout all of the texts of Hinduism; in fact, their stories are often quite different, depending upon which translation of the text one uses. For example, some may state that a girl must always put her father or husband first, worshipping the husband as a god; while other sections or translations talk about women in military positions or as traveling scholars, holding their equal with male believers.

In Hinduism, the creator god is the Brahman, the imperial Absolute, who has no gender. One of the leaders worshipped by Hindus is the female goddess Durga. She is the mother-protector, often depicted with eight to eighteen arms (each holding something significant), and she is able to battle any threats from any direction. A true leader whose left eye "represents desire, symbolized by the moon; her right eye represents action, symbolized by the sun; and her middle eye stands for knowledge, symbolized by fire."[84]

Of the things she carries, some of the most significant to Hinduism are the conch shell, the bow and arrows, the lotus, and the thunderbolt. The shell represents the mystic word *om*, the sound that holds her to God; the bow and arrows represent energy and her power over present and possible dangers; the lotus is literally born in mud, thus Durga's hold on it reminds all that everything beautiful and worthwhile is rooted in struggle; and the

---

83. Bhishma, Mahabharata 13.47.26
84. Rajhans, "The Goddess Durga."

thunderbolt is a reminder to attack challenges rather than to walk away without trying.

Though the Goddess Mother Durga has 108 names and many incarnations, one thing is certain: she represents courage and determination, very powerful qualities for women to embody.

Other divine feminine leaders exist as well, though they might not be worshipped as deities. For example, in the Biblical book of Judith, her story begins amidst a war, and though Judith herself is a widow described as "pious," she is quick to prove her willingness to do whatever is necessary for the nation of Israel, including lying and cheating. With a great deal of courage and the belief that God would protect her, Judith seduced Holofernes, one of Nebuchadnezzar's generals and the man who has laid siege to her town of Bethulia. Wielding her own sword, she cut his head off, and that act stopped the war. Though she has essentially taken on the characteristics of a male warrior and saved her town, she returns to the life she led before as a pious widow, and lives past the ripe old age of 100. In other words, she did what she needed to do in order to stop the war, then returned to serving her community rather than to take advantage of the opportunity to subjugate the people she'd just saved.

In Greek mythology, Athena represents the love of education and of succeeding. Jean Shinonda Bolen states "your love of reading and science revealed Athena, the Goddess of Wise Strategy and Crafts, stirring within you."[85] She is known to be wise and strategic, two important traits for women to have if they want to succeed in business. A stern-looking goddess, she emanates authority and wisdom. Even the gods were known to ask Athena's advice.

In the Mormon religion, the fourth largest church in the United States, women are considered equal to men as leaders, though it's the men who hold the priesthood. According to the church, the women's roles as caretakers and child-raisers are equivalent to the roles of the men in the priesthood (Mormon).

---

85. Bolen, "Discover Your Signature Goddesses."

In short, women who want to lead in any philosophy have an upward battle to prove not only their worthiness but to prove themselves better in some ways than the men they would either replace or join as equal partners.

Managing People from a Divine Feminine Perspective

One of the reasons women have traditionally experienced a slower and more difficult road to success than men who are in the same positions is that women's desires and needs have been purported to be less important than men's are.

People who cry are usually considered soft, especially in the workplace. Supervisors who offer a touch of comfort are caught between being compassionate and invasive, especially depending upon whether they define as masculine or feminine. The more encouraging and nurturing type of leadership is often seen as ineffective. I'm sure you can see a pattern here. In order to succeed, there needs to be a balance of traits in any leader.

The United Nations Commission on the Status of Women states in its 2018 International Day of Rural Women article that 43 percent of the workforce in developing rural countries is made up of women, and they are also responsible for collecting 80 percent of the water needed for their communities to survive.[86] The unhealthy living conditions and cooking practices results in six out of ten of the premature deaths of the women themselves, as well as family members. The UN Commission fights for the infrastructure and education necessary for these women to raise their families safely, and to provide a healthier lifestyle (UN Women statement). The reason? The women are running those communities. She who has the water has the power. With some education and skills, these women are invincible, and I would be willing to place a bet that the more educated the women are, the better those communities will become. I predict some strong female leaders rising through the ranks in those countries—humane, thoughtful leaders who know how to work within communities.

---

86. United Nations, "International Day of Rural Women."

In the United States in 2018, though more women than ever ran for public office, the number of women CEOs for Fortune 500 companies dropped by 25 percent.[87] That sounds like a huge drop until you consider the actual numbers: from thirty-two women CEOs to twenty-seven. That's only a five person drop, but it's also a small percentage of the total number of CEOs (twenty-seven women out of a total of five hundred) In fact, CNBC reported in May of 2018 that twelve of the companies on the list had no female board members.

In her article, Stewart suggests that the reason more women are running for office rather than adding to the number holding high office in the corporate world is that those women entering politics don't have to take the time to climb the corporate ladder. Instead, they can jump into the race, even if they don't have party backing. In the business world, you can't immediately jump to the head of the line, and if you're a woman, chances are good that you will be passed by several times for a promotion before finally attaining your goal.

Marilyn Nyborg states: "A recent study showed in corporations that men ARE embracing feminine responses in their management styles quite successfully. While at the same time women continue to be seen as weak when they come from their innate modes of operating."[88]

Ironically, certain businesses boast a workforce that's primarily female. Take, for example, publishing. A 2016 survey that the publisher Lee and Low conducted showed that "78 percent of publishing staff overall were female. At executive or board level, however, 40 percent of respondents identified as men."[89] The whole top tier at publishing companies is usually dominated by men, but the other nine-tenths of the organization is run by smart and savvy women. Women are usually the ones buying the manuscripts that turn into books, marketing them, publicizing them, and ensuring that they turn a profit, but the big bucks at the top are still going to men.

The same phenomenon happens in the movie industry. Within the past decade there has been a very noticeable shift from a sizeable majority

87. Stewart, "Women Are Running for Office in Record Numbers."
88. Nyborg, "Turning the World Right Side Up."
89. Lee and Low, The Diversity Baseline Survey.

of white men being in control of major studios to a few brave and talented women who are creating award-winning and artistically creative films.

The stories that have come from the #metoo and #ownvoices movements encourage more people to share those, spawning creativity from everyone in the arts, and I predict a tidal wave of books and movies in this vein within the next couple of years. (It's about time.) I strongly suspect a lot of those stories will open doors for people like the goddess Athena or strong women like Durga.

When I think of the divine feminine in an office, I can't help but think of Oprah. She recognizes the spirit in everyone, encourages the intimate communication that reveals a person's true heart, and has the insight—the positive and strong insight—to create a business that has produced a lot of plain ol' good. She has empowered many, has given in ways anyone with her amount of money should, and respects the land and its animals. In business, she is the strongest role model of the divine feminine that I can think of. Women who see themselves in top-level corporations would be wise to study how Oprah built hers.

Men who embrace the same techniques are said to "manage successfully" while women are seen as weak. Oprah is able to balance and to combine masculine and feminine strengths. She's capable of making tough decisions, but also knows when to build schools. She's artistic, yet possesses the ability to organize and to manage her time efficiently. She hasn't let the trials of her life defeat her, but she's also not brittle as a result of the experiences.

Though Elizabeth Gilbert, the bestselling author of *Eat, Pray, Love,* is not a CEO, she could have been referring to Oprah when she said, "The women whom I love and admire for their strength and grace did not get that way because shit worked out. They got that way because shit went wrong, and they handled it. They handled it in a thousand different ways on a thousand different days, but they handled it. Those women are my superheroes."[90]

---

90. Gilbert, "Wisdom & Age & Women," *ElizabethGilbert,* June 22, 2014.

Reese Witherspoon once said, "Ambition is not a dirty word," meaning that women shouldn't be ashamed of wanting more from life. If you have the urge to succeed, dig for some of Athena's wisdom or for the biblical Judith's courage. It's there. Right there, inside you.

My Story: Riding the Amtrak

In 2017, I had an informal conversation with a woman in an Amtrak train station during my trip across the United States. She said, "We had duties, we women, when I was a child in Bangladesh. As a child, my father protected me. Traditionally, I did not receive an academic education. My job was to preserve the social and cultural values learned at home. That was considered quite important for us as women. As a wife, I was protected by my husband, and I had parental responsibilities. Very important. Then my husband died, and I went to school. If I had been an elderly widow, I would be protected by my eldest son. Elders are treated with respect and opinions on family issues are requested by the young ones. But my children are young, so I'm lucky to have this freedom to attend school."

We'd been talking about life. I'd told her that I'd been an academic dean, that I'd retired early, and taken the chance that I could make a living at writing, as I had for so many years before the world of education consumed me. She was surprised that I'd held a position like that (probably because as we sat there talking, I wore a bulging backpack, dirty jeans, and multicolored sneakers). We spent a good fifteen minutes talking about a working mother's struggles to educate herself. Enrolled in engineering school, she had the primary duty to care for her two young children, as well. I nodded. I'd gone back to college as a single mother, and I didn't graduate from college until I was an empty-nester.

We talked until I had to run to catch my Amtrak to points further west, but our conversation echoed in my mind for a long time afterward. I reflected on the jobs I'd had and the managers/deans/vice presidents who'd shared their wisdom along the way. Most of them had been men. Some of them taught me valuable lessons about managing people simply by what they did poorly. Some of them actually taught me valuable lessons about managing people well. But by the time I was ready to retire, I'd finally begun managing the way that I felt comfortable. I'd taken all the advice I received from men, I'd watched the very few female bosses I'd had, and I had settled my own Buddhist philosophy. Right or wrong, strong or not, I managed from a position of respect and a compassion for those I worked with, and I tried to remember to glance at the poster on my desk whenever I needed to be grounded. The framed little poster included a line from each of the world's religions, all of which said basically the same thing: treat everyone else the way you'd like to be treated.

Reflection

British socialist, theosophist, and activist for women's rights Annie Besant worked tirelessly for the causes in which she passionately believed. Ahead of her time (she was born in 1847 and died in 1933), she wrote stories and children's books (even though her husband took all her earnings), fought against what she believed were the injustices of the world, and actively engaged with politics in both the United Kingdom and India.

In this quote, she discusses a goddess who represents the ultimate in leadership in the United States, literally leading thousands of people onto this country's shores where they believed they might achieve the ultimate in success.

> *Liberty is a great celestial goddess, strong, beneficent, and austere, and she can never descend upon a nation by the shouting of crowds, nor by arguments of unbridled passion, nor by the hatred of class against class.*[91]
> ~Annie Besant

Though Lady Liberty is said to be more of a metaphor or symbol than a goddess, Besant writes here that Liberty can only exist when the people above whom she reigns quietly observe her and her expectations. This goddess, in

---

91. Besant, "The Changing World."

charge of fairness for all, is shown as "strong" (normally a male trait), "benef-icent" (a term usually used for kings), and "austere" (a term that often is a negative description of a woman). When you think of offering someone lib-erty (or of Lady Liberty herself), what comes to mind? Describe in detail what this word means to you.

Practice: Time to Meditate

When you're climbing the corporate ladder or carving out a space for your new small business, it's important to keep your eye on the goal. One of the ways to do this is to meditate. Try this simple focusing mediation as often as you can—or whenever you feel yourself doubting your ability to continue placing one foot in front of the other on your path to success. Be patient with yourself. Nothing happens overnight (even though some people appear to have an overnight success, there is always years of invisible hard work behind the scenes).

- Carve out five minutes a day for yourself. Perhaps it's the end of your lunch break or the first five minutes before you fall asleep. Save that time for yourself.
- Find a comfortable and quiet space, sitting or lying down.
- Breathe deeply, counting your inhalations and exhalations until you find your body settling.
- Keep a positive image of yourself in your mind. Imagine yourself in the position you want to achieve. See yourself happy, strong, and successful. Breathe that image into your heart.
- See your favorite goddess sitting behind your shoulder, supporting you, offering compassion and love.
- Hold that image and continue breathing, slowly and calmly, then offer your thanks to your goddess guide.
- Bring yourself out of your meditation with the intention to bring that light and power with you into your day/evening.

The more often you conduct a simple five-minute meditation like this one, the more natural it will become, and the more quickly you'll be able to arrive at that peaceful place where you can fully achieve your objective.

Main Takeaways from This Chapter

- Discussing the female teachers, scholars, gurus, and managers
- Assessing women in the workforce
- Researching the goddesses who inspire us to succeed

The Goddesses

Sarasvati (Hindu), goddess of creative education

Cybele (ancient Phrygia), goddess of fertility and protectress in time of war

Mother Mary (Christian), mother of Jesus

Auset (Egyptian), mother goddess

Kali (Hindu), goddess of time, change, and destruction

Storm (African), fictional superhero

Malala Yousafzai (Pakistani), activist for female education

Harriet Jacobs (African American), activist for slave education

Ozwiena (Slavic), goddess of gossip

Chapter Ten

The Strength of Fireside Tales and Clothesline Chats

One of the things I know for sure about my divinely feminine friends is that most of us have the ability to hold a conversation that goes late into the night. We talk about family or friends, current politics or the latest movies, about our emotions and our fears, and about absolutely nothing at all.

Comedians have created stereotypes of women talking and talking and talking. Why is that funny? I believe that communication is a power that women employ with an intuitive sense, and they know when to pause during their day to honestly inquire of their friends/family, "Are you okay?" It's invaluable that mothers can tell when something is wrong with their progeny (dog and cat and horse mothers belong in this group, too). How many lives have been saved due to a mother's intuition? And with her ability to talk to a person—really deeply and intimately?

We often don't give value to those everyday talks, the chats beside the fire late at night when one- or two-word sentences is all you need, and the quick whispers at the clothesline when that is the only place where you're safe. Fizza Imitaz, one of my interviewees, pointed out that her mother was her first religious teacher, but she was later replaced by a Hafiz Gee, a gentleman who came to the home to teach Fizza and her siblings how to read the Quran and how to recite the Namaz. I wonder how many of those first lessons Fizza's mother delivered while they were washing dishes or doing similar household chores.

A while ago, I reviewed a play starring the mom of a former instructor of mine. The instructor comes from an exceptionally talented family, and I knew of his mother, a Grammy-award-winning singer, but I hadn't seen her in performance. *The Clothesline Muse* had me nodding with recognition by the end of the first ten minutes. Its central metaphor (that clothesline) was the lifeline for the characters in the tale, women related by blood as well as by the community of washerwomen. It's a story of the struggle of African American women, though I saw shadows of my own female ancestors in the stories, as well. There was a time when most women spent part of their day hanging clothes on the line in the backyard to dry, often seeing their friends in those backyards doing the same.

History happened over the clothesline. News passed from household to household, an early version of Facebook. Diagnoses were made of childhood illnesses, and cures were offered. Recipes were exchanged, seeds were swapped, and support was offered. Most importantly, however, was that the clothesline held the women together, often during enormous distress: the bonds of slavery, back-breaking menial work, and the heartache of struggling for the right to be. To just *be*.

Those stories women shared, never as respected as the conversations of men, could save lives. Those fireside chats, clothesline talks, or afternoon teas have always been the underground communication that links the family to the community, to the next town, and to the outside world. They are not only just as important, but even more so.

As Alexandria Ocasio-Cortez, a New York Congresswoman, said in a recent tweet: "Ever wonder how expression that's feminine, working-class, queer, or PoC isn't deemed as having 'gravitas,' but talking like an Aaron Sorkin character does? Men have 'gravitas,' women get 'likeable.'"[92]

The Goddesses as Teachers

Sarasvati is one of my favorite goddesses. She comes from the Hindu faith and represents education (learning, knowledge, wisdom), as well as music and art. Basically, she's the goddess of creative people. In early carvings and statues, she's depicted as a large breasted, four-armed woman surrounded by other women in the arts. In more contemporary representations, she's a

---

92. Alexandria Ocasio Cortez, https://twitter.com/aoc/status/1087093156397678593?lang=en.

dark-haired beauty who holds a stringed instrument on her lap and several folded documents in one of her hands. Often, a large bird, such as a swan or peacock, is pictured with her. A vital member of the Hindu trinity, she holds the place of Shakti of the Brahma, the First Person of the trinity, and is often called the Divine Mother. As the giver of language to the universe, her power cannot be denied, for without language, what is a human being?

People taking examinations are likely to invoke Sarasvati's name and to ask her for help in successfully passing those exams.

In a matrilineal society, such as the Aboriginal in Australia, people are valued for being cooperative, while other societies (particularly European) that are patriarchal value domination.[93] Being cooperative means being able to communicate, as well.

Yet, even though the Aboriginal society itself is matrilineal, the Australian culture as a whole is not; thus Aboriginal women struggle every day. Political activists who are Aboriginal women are shut down, forbidden to share their viewpoints, and taunted and threatened, sometimes with death.

In the Bible, Jephthah's unnamed daughter was to be sacrificed. She asked for a two-month reprieve in order to see family and friends. Though it is argued in theological communities about whether Jephthah did, indeed, sacrifice his daughter, there was a memorial held every year to commemorate her death and women lamented for four days.

In an article written for the Jewish Women's Archive, Karla Bombach wonders about the woman's female relatives, why they weren't mentioned, what they might have done to help the girl, and finally, whether the killing actually took place. She asks: "Finally, what is the function of this story in the biblical text? Some suggest that it is meant to point up the rash and foolish behavior of Jephthah. But his unconscionable behavior would also have been a sign of Israel's depravity and thus an argument for instituting monarchical rule, presumably a more stable and upright form of government than what is currently in place. This message is here mediated primarily through the

93. Hartmann, "Her Story."

victimization of a woman. Women's lives and reproductive potential were essential for community and family survival. The loss of the daughter perhaps represents, in dramatic form, the dangers (amid apparent success) of the leadership of the judges. As a potential mother, the daughter represents the future for family and community."[94]

Again, we are pointed to that most precious of female attributes: the ability to add members to her community. But why would her story be so briefly told? Why would the story of Job and his son be more complete?

One of the reasons I'm including this story in this chapter is because the way this story is communicated leaves out important details about the sacrificed woman—like her name. In this case, when details like that are left out, the communication—albeit silent—is that the woman is not important enough to name.

In several books of the Bible, it is clear that women are not meant to voice their thoughts or feelings. In fact, Timothy states, "Let a woman learn in silence with all submissiveness. I permit no woman to teach or to have authority over men, she is to keep silent."[95]

Ironically, the woman is the first teacher in most families, notwithstanding culture, era, or religion. If that woman is remanded to silence, the children will not learn and if a generation doesn't learn, nations suffer.

Cybele, the "mother goddess" of the ancient land of Phrygia, part of Anatolia (what is now Turkey), appears to be the only goddess/god from that area of the world. Temples built to worship Cybele pre-date Christianity in Asia Minor, and her image resulted in the Church being identified as female throughout early Christian communities. The way the Virgin Mary was worshipped often mimics the ways Cybele was worshipped as the Great Mother.[96]

Ross Sheppard Kraemer states that "women who played cultic leadership roles in pagan contexts would have expected to play such roles in their new-found Christianity as well."

---

94. Bohmbach, "Daughter of Jephthah."
95. 1 Timothy 2:11–14, King James Version.
96. Kraemer, *Her Share of the Blessings.*

As a partial result of Cybele- and Mary-worship, women in this region held considerable authority, and many women followed both of these women, finding a religious world represented by these two important feminine figures. However, Kraemer points out that once Tertullian (a Tunisian/Berber author who produced books of Latin-Christian theology) began to write, he expressed explicit rules about "forbidding women to baptize, teach, and have authority over men: even when he describes a woman prophet, he emphasizes the precautions taken to assure that her prophecy does not violate any of these restrictions."

I wonder if Cybele would agree with his rules.

In the fourth century, *The Constitutions of the Holy Apostles* lays out the appropriate way for widows to behave. Not only widows, however. The *Constitutions* states how people should behave in church, where they should sit, and states that women cannot teach in church but that they could pray and listen. Women were to be meek, passive, obedient, and to stay home doing the housecleaning, cooking, spinning, and weaving. And women should not prophesy. In other words, if a woman's intuition warned her that something might happen, she was to keep it to herself.

It is in the *Constitutions* that we see the first indication of the ways women lived and how they should be grouped as virgins, unmarried women, or widows.

Anne Lamott, a novelist and nonfiction author, talks about taking her teenaged son to church in her memoir, *Plan B: Further Thoughts on Faith*. None of his friends attends a church, temple, mosque, or hall. He can't completely resist her, since she's giving him a roof over his head and food to eat, though he senses something. "While I can feel Sam's agonized resistance to attending church, I know there is nourishment for him there—there is real teaching—and a prime parental role is to insist that your kid get real teaching."[97]

I can think of many contemporary women who have acted nobly or compassionately, women who might not be associated with any religious group but have had the purest of intentions. Some of those women are mentioned in an article by Melissa Carver for the Chopra Center entitled "Ten Female

---

97. Lamott, *Plan B*, 196.

Archetypes and Leaders to Inspire You." Women like Princess Diana, who the article says maintained "a solid stance of motherhood to not only her own boys but also to the world," is included, along with Biblical women like Mother Mary, and mythological women, such as the Egyptian mother goddess, Auset, and the Hindu goddess of time, change, and destruction, Kali. They point out that Auset can teach us the benefits of good nutrition, while Kali reminds us to let go of destructive emotions. Those are two elements we all need.

Carver also includes superheroes in her list, such as Storm, who descended from a line of African princesses, and Mystique, a shape-shifting mutant. If we look at what Storm can teach us, it's that her powers are a direct result of any spikes of emotion. Whenever she's upset, she causes some serious damage. To me, that states that what we think, we will become. If we allow anger to control us, we become an angry person. If we think of what we want rather than what we don't want, we keep negativity out of the equation and often get what we want from life. Try using a positive statement instead of a not/no/nothing statement when faced with an issue you must overcome. You might not be able to control the weather like Storm, but you will be able to control your reactions.

Mystique, on the other hand, can mimic anything's appearance, a skill that we might adopt when entering a situation where we are out of our comfort zone. Instead of feeling out of place, imagine yourself channeling Mystique's ability to change to fit the situation. I'm not suggesting you become a chameleon, but that you learn to adapt. If you change the way you react in any given situation, the situation will change, as well.

And, finally, Carver mentions Oprah Winfrey, stating that "her strength, passion, determination and giving spirit"[98] draws people to her, and that her perseverance is a character trait that most people should adopt. Her positive thinking and spirituality have brought her through many tough situations and made her the influential person she is today. Her many followers would agree that adopting those traits can make a difference in your life.

---

98. Carver, "10 Female Archetypes and Leaders to Inspire You."

Certainly, we must add Malala Yousafzai, the youngest woman to be nominated for a Nobel Peace Prize, to the list of contemporary women whose voices are making a peaceful difference in the world around them. Malala's goal is that, during her lifetime, every girl has the freedom to attend school.[99]

Malala began voicing her wish for girls in her part of Pakistan to have the right to an education after the Taliban took control of her village and her father's school for girls. But her strong voice and the support she aroused made her a target. An attacker shot her on the left side of her head, immediately bringing global support for her recovery. After she recovered, she and her father built a fund called the Malala Fund, and she travels constantly to speak about ensuring that the girls who are still uneducated be given that opportunity to learn.

Balancing the Scales

"In *Half the Sky*, journalists Bernard Krisher and Sherryl WuDunn, talk about education from a different viewpoint. They discuss how the lack of education often leads girls into horrible situations, such as being trapped in the sex slave trade or being openly snatched from shopping malls. The best way to save them, the authors say, is to keep the girls in school, which not only keeps them safe from trafficking but also provides the education girls need to spot situations they need to avoid."[100]

Keeping people uneducated has historically been the way cultures have kept certain members of society in check for thousands of years. Depriving a people of an education ensures they will rely on you for everything, giving you total control. Think about slavery and how those enslaved had to keep their own education a secret from their enslavers. Education is power, especially for women, and that power can not only keep them safe but also affords them the ability to provide their own support, no longer having to rely on others (such as men or slave owners).

---

99. Malala.org, the official website of Malala Yousafzai.
100. Kristoff and WuDunn, *Half the Sky*.

In the United States, one former slave, Harriet Jacobs, used her illegally gotten education to write *Life of a Slave Girl*, a treatise that depicted the cruelty she underwent throughout her life, and her story opened the doors for many others to realize they could do the same. Her courage and intelligence provided evidence for those fighting against slavery and her tale became the defining text for how African American women lived pre–Civil War. Thanks to her incredible bravery and her perseverance, other women of her era recognized the value of education.

One of the first times I spoke about what I was discovering as I researched this book was at a library function where I met with a group of about thirty people, only four of whom were male, and two of those were children. While I talked about women recognizing the divine in themselves, one woman turned and apologized to the man who sat next to her—as though recognizing our own worth in the divine would diminish his and would make us guilty of being man-haters. Basically, she was asking permission to be good, powerful, happy, loving, compassionate, and independent. Divine. Feminine.

Further, she was asking for permission to *speak* about it.

Why do we feel the need to apologize for being our best and strongest selves? Do masculine people beg our pardon for their power?

Powerful Women and Communication

The connection between powerful women, education, and communication is as old as the religious theories themselves. In Christine de Pizan's *The Book of the City of Ladies*, first published in 1410, she states that a woman invented the Latin alphabet and, therefore, began the idea of formal education. In addition to conducting a conversation with the three women who personified the virtues of Reason, Rectitude, and Justice, the book celebrates women as a whole, and all of their accomplishments. She cautions that to "try to turn something which is good and praiseworthy in a woman—her tenderness—into something bad and blameworthy" is wicked and closed-minded and continues to support women by stating that they have a "natural instinct to be gentle."[101]

A more contemporary version of the power of women communicating directly to one other is a special moment in history when two of the world's most powerful countries (England and Germany) were led by two of the most powerful prime ministers in history: Theresa May and Angela Merkel. More than two dozen women lead countries throughout the world (given any particular moment and election timing). Not surprisingly, those numbers have been fairly stagnant. Think about the Middle Ages in Europe and how many women ruled as queens (or their equivalent). A quick look shows at least a dozen or more, which is only eight short of the approximate twenty-plus that we can see in today's world.

If the room was full of women leaders, what type of changes might we see in governments, education, finances, or defense? I suggest that we might see more schools being built, and fewer weapons of mass destruction.

Intuition

Author Sophie Bashford urges us to recognize the intuitive sense that is inside all of us. She says, "it is a sense that bypasses the mind, or 'lower self.' It is sometimes called your 'sixth sense,' because it transcends the physical or mental planes."[102] We often don't think of intuition as being education or communication because of that transcendence, but perhaps that type of knowledge is downgraded because women are more likely to accept that intuition than the masculine among us.

I remember my father tenderly teasing my mother, saying she had "witchy tendencies." He was convinced that she had some kind of extra-sensory talents that were unexplainable, because he did not understand them. He attributed her abilities to a magical or otherworldly power, though my mother was the least likely person to be drawn to the metaphysical. I can

---

101. De Pizan, *The Book of the City of Ladies.*
102. Bashford, https://www.sophiebashford.com/5-steps-to-awakening-divine-feminine-energy/.

vouch for her ability to know when we'd done something wrong (though I suspect all mothers basically know that about their kids, right?), but she also knew when something was going to happen or when a family member might need help or a deep conversation before they even reached out.

Now that I can appreciate the difference between someone who has intuition and someone who might have an empathetic sense that we struggle to explain, I believe my mother knew how to read people, especially those she loved, and knew to trust her gut instinct or intuition. That's a talent few have, but she had it in abundance.

I notice that women doubt their gut instincts most of the time. I also notice that we say "maybe" or "perhaps" much more than men do. I call my writing students on that, especially when they're trying to make a point. *Go in and make a statement*, I tell them. *Put a point on that pencil and stab it right into the heart of the argument.* The male writers get it, but I see the writers who identify as female hesitating. They doubt themselves. I realize my mother didn't doubt herself, which is probably why she was so good at picking up on what wasn't said.

My mother taught me it was okay to be a strong woman, and I admit that is the one thing everyone says about me, but I still don't trust my gut instinct, my feminine intuition, as much as I should. I remember getting into a car with a man I had recently met and feeling a strange tightness in the middle of my stomach. Only moments later, he pulled down a side road, locked the doors, and tried to convince me to have sex with him. Luckily, I was able to open the door and ran back down to the intersection. It was enough for him to get the message, but it would have been much easier if I'd just trusted my gut instinct in the first place

We should honor our intuitive impulses, remembering that it is a power that comes from our emotions rather than our intellect. Celebrate that energy we have within us and trust that it will keep you safe.

In Sue Monk Kidd's *Dance of the Dissident Daughter*, she points out that she believes "women must have the whale's instinct." Basically, what she's saying is that when we sense something is coming that might be rough or dangerous, we should "send out our vibrations, our stories, so that no one gets lost."[103] When was the last time you felt like something was going on but couldn't put your finger on it? Sit with that feeling for a moment and pay attention to what comes up. You might thank yourself later.

During the #metoo movement, we shared our stories, told others about our instincts, and even though we might never have the statistics, I'd be willing to bet my last dime that those stories saved some women from getting caught in the same trap—or even better: taught them how to trust their own instincts. This is where communication naturally leads to self-education.

Like Kidd stated, we sent out our vibrations so no one would get lost.

My Story: Peeking Behind the Curtain— Reading Women's Journals

During my MFA studies at Vermont College, my research centered on women writers and their public and private voices. I read the journals of dozens of famous female authors, as well as their published fiction, essays, or poetry. Many of the women spoke of their relationships with men or their lack thereof. Mary Shelley shared her journal with her husband; Virginia Woolf longed for a room of her own where she could write without her husband (an editor); Anaïs Nin found ways to live with men and still remain somewhat independent; and May Sarton simply decided that she would rather live with women.

I continued to study the different way writers communicate in my PhD program at the Union Institute and University. I widened my scope of study this time, looking instead at transgender authors and their written voices pre- and post-transition. To be honest, I expected to find a difference and to have my results mirror somewhat the results I'd seen during my MFA research: that the public written voice is quite different from the private one, even to the point of sentence structure. Instead, the written voice of transgender authors was the same, both before and after their transition to their

---

103. Kidd, *The Dance of the Dissident Daughter*, 2.

self-identified gender. The written word is as an identifying marker, as clear as fingerprints.

In one aspect, my two studies mirror each other: each of the writers I studied at one point or another discussed her/his own personal journey in a spiritual manner. The discussion might have been the central theme of a major work of literature (as with Mary Shelley's *Frankenstein*, which is ultimately her grappling with science versus religion) or it might be buried within the perfectly structured lines of a poem, as is the case with May Sarton. Her poetry and memoirs circle back to her own spiritual journey many times. She examines her life and communicates it in poetry that reflects the divine feminine joy of nature or the minutest moments of the day when love reveals itself in the smallest ways.

To me, using a journal to record how I feel about my day or about my work, or to keep one to note what I see and hear in places I've never visited before, or to create a journal of memories to be passed along to future generations, is a way of communicating in a feminine way about the human moments. How much did the baby grow since last week? What's the best way to get rid of spider mites in the garden? Why is it so frustrating to convince a ten-year-old you know what you're talking about? What's the best time of day to photograph the Eiffel Tower, and hey, what was the name of that coffee place around the corner? The one where you can sit outside and watch the world go by?

Whether the journals are full of pithy details of ramblings through London, as Woolf did so well, or reminiscences of a heartbreakingly passionate relationship with God, as Flannery O'Connor's journal was, communicating on the page to an unseen reader, possibly a family member who might find the writings in the future, journals offer an inside view into a life, using one of the most divine methods of communication: writing to the self.

Reflection

When we discuss the way people communicate, as well as the way they receive education, we discover that vast differences still exist between the feminine and the masculine. Ozwiena is a very different kind of divine feminine, a Slavic goddess that is associated with echoes and/or gossip. She's unable to keep a secret. Often that can be dangerous, for both the secret giver as well as the secret holder. The lessons taught when one is aware that the precious secret one has entrusted to another has been released to the world might educate both people in a rather painful manner. In Niki Lemut's quote below, she describes the goddess of gossip as being unable to control herself.

> *"As the goddess of gossip, Ozwiena was unable to keep*
> *any secret or private conversation. If she disliked somebody,*
> *she distorted the meaning of his words."*[104]
> ~Niki Lemut

We all know someone like Ozwiena. In your writing about this quote, think about how painful it might be to be unable to keep a secret. Could there be some guilt? Some self-abuse? A debilitating doubt? Were you one of those people who got into trouble for speaking up? Do you believe women are kept quiet? What could you learn about gossip from an experience with someone like Ozwiena?

Practice: Being Mindful

In Buddhism, one learns how to walk mindfully, think mindfully, conduct simple household chores mindfully, and to speak mindfully. What does that mean? It means anchoring yourself in the present moment and appreciating everything that happens in that moment rather than obsessing about something that happened in the past or wondering what's going to happen in the future. What mindfulness does for you as a human being is that it connects you with yourself, as well as with others, in a way that might provide more insight—or inflict less pain than we might if we think/do/act without taking a moment to be in the moment.

Here's a simple way of speaking mindfully:

---

104. Lemut, *Ozwiena's Echo.*

- Slow down. Have you ever noticed that you might have more accidents when you're in a rush? Not just in the car, but in the kitchen or even when getting ready for work. Take your time. Be mindful of everything you're doing and try not to rush, even if you're late. Chances are, you'll save more time and energy. Employ this whenever you're about to enter into a conversation. Slow down a minute. Take a breath.

- Before speaking: whether you're talking to a child, an adult, a parent, or an employer, before you begin speaking, take a look at that person. Think about what kind of moment they might be having and how you could calmly and patiently speak to that person *before* opening your mouth to begin the conversation.

- When speaking: breathe deeply and take your time to choose your words carefully. Pause after the other person speaks before you answer them. Think about how to respond in a manner that does not start conflict, yet still speaks about how you feel.

- After speaking: once the conversation/dialogue is finished, take another moment to inhale and exhale, summing up the conversation in your mind. Smile as you do so. Fold your hands in your lap. Breathe peace into your body, even if the conversation was contentious. Inhale and exhale as many times as necessary for the conflict within to calm down before you move to the next task.

Main Takeaways from This Chapter

- Defining the feminine power of communication
- Listening when a goddess speaks
- Opening the fireside/clothesline talks and stepping into education
- Investigating different types of communication

Chapter Eleven

The Wisdom of Feminine Creatives

In Twyla Tharp's book *The Creative Habit,* she points out that we are all born with strands of what she calls "creative code" hardwired into our bodies.[105] Creativity is part of our DNA. As an award-winning dancer/choreographer, world renowned for her style, Tharp knows about creativity. In other parts of her book, she points out that it takes a great deal of courage to face that creative part of ourselves, and that is probably one of the reasons why there's so much respect given to those who can create and earn a living doing so. But what's even more important than that courage is the ability to be a goal-setter, to be able to organize the actions needed to reach those goals, and the tenacity it takes to perfect one's technique.

That tenacity arises from motivation, which is a factor that Albert Rothenberg, author of *Creativity & Madness,* believes is common in every single creative. He points out that "[c]reative people are extraordinarily highly motivated, both to work and to produce, but, more than that, they are motivated to produce entities that are both new and valuable—creations."[106]

Rothenberg talks about specific creatives (both in the arts, as well as the sciences) and how their psychological process might push them toward madness. However, it is interesting to note that the female creatives he chooses to highlight in this book as having psychological problems (subtitled, by the way, "New Findings and Old Stereotypes") are people that other authors have labeled geniuses or groundbreakers.

In *Creativity* by Mikhail Csikszentmihalyi, one of the sections deals with the freedom one needs as a creative in order to try and fail (sometimes repeatedly). He makes a point that he'd asked his research respondents to

---

105. Tharp, *The Creative Habit.*
106. Rothenberg, *Creativity & Madness.*

The Goddesses

Aphrodite (Greek), goddess of love, beauty, and creativity

Hathor (Egyptian), goddess of music, dance, joy, love, sexuality, and maternal care

Sarasvati (Hindu), goddess of knowledge and the arts

Maîtresse Mambo Erzulie Fréda (also called Mater Dolorosa) (Haitian Vodou), spirit of love, beauty, dance

Berizaiten (Japanese Buddhist), patron goddess of literature, music, wealth, and femininity

Brigid (Celtic), goddess of spring, fertility, poetry, and smithcraft

Calliope (Greek), goddess of epic poetry

Clio (Greek), goddess protector of history

Erato (Greek), goddess personification of lyric history

Enterpe (Greek), goddess of song and elegiac poetry

Melpomene (Greek), goddess of tragic performances

Polyhymnia (Greek), goddess personifying hymns

Terpsichore (Greek), goddess representing dance

Thalia (Greek), goddess of comedy

Urama (Greek), goddess of astronomy

answer questions about what might have aided their creative process. Many of them said their spouses and families gave them both the freedom and support necessary for the creative process to spread their wings. Csikszentmihalyi's belief is that instead of proving creative people are flighty and less likely to be involved in promiscuity, the answers proved just the opposite. So many of the individuals he questioned were in lasting exclusive relationships that supported their art that Csikszentmihalyi stated that might be the norm for those who focus on their creativities.[107]

The researchers I've mentioned describe creatives as having an interest in the art that starts in childhood and is nurtured, educated, and promoted throughout adulthood. It is easy to state here that it's hard for most creatives to find support to follow their passion, especially when that passion might not be producing income. It's twice as hard for women to follow that passion when, in some cases, education is not readily available and, in other cases, the support of family and friends is nonexistent.

The art of creating a new object is equivalent to giving birth. One takes a part of one's life or body, reshapes it, gives it spirit, and sends it off into the world, hoping it'll do well. At times, at least in my experience, the literary world actually mimics the time sequence of birth: the actual germinal period, that time when the design for the art is still in the artist's mind, varies, depending upon the artist. Some writers take a decade to write a book, while others can spit one out in a month. Some artists create a painting in a night, while others might still be touching up several years later. But once that germ of a literary idea is delivered to the editor, goes through the editing process, and is developed into a printed project, it's nine months or more before the book is on a bookstore shelf.

I've spent a lot of time pondering creativity throughout my life, and because most of my friends are in the arts or on the fringes, I have had plenty of opportunity to observe creative people, most of whom are women. To be honest, this is one area where I see a lot of similarities among the genders: the

---

107. Csikszentmihalyi, *Creativity*.

way creative people produce their work, how they see themselves, and how they work in societies around them. Divine feminine people dance, as Anne Lamott says: "with a banged-up heart. You dance to the absurdities of life; you dance to the minuet of old friendships."[108]

Creatives tend to be thoughtful people who sit to the side, watching the other, more gregarious members of the group interact. They are introverted extraverts, people who are okay in groups but need to recharge their batteries alone—and they're quite comfortable being alone. They are passionate people, each and every one of them, and they are knowledge-seekers. It doesn't matter if they are writers, sculptors, dancers, or musicians; every creative person I know is full of information—often about topics quite different from the work they produce. It's a natural curiosity that all creatives have.

So, how does creativity relate to the divine feminine if I've just said that I've found most creative people—no matter the gender—to be similar to each other? Because for too many years the creativity of women was silenced. Women artists couldn't compete in worldwide awards. Females were often told to put down the pen or the brush or the hammer. Up until the early 1800s, a female's education was considered both unnecessary and "improper."

In Mary Wollstonecraft's famous essay, *A Vindication of the Rights of Women*,[109] she challenges the status quo by asking why women were on the outskirts of education. Within the treatise, she proposes a link between public and private education, largely defining the public school system, but even more importantly, putting all genders in the same classrooms. In other parts of the treatise, she discusses the lack of education for women, proposing that denying a woman education might result in her retaliation. In other words, she warned very clearly that if the patriarchy didn't wise up and soon, they'd be paying a price.

Wollstonecraft thought deeply about the world around her and her place within it, and though her life ended in childbirth, the baby daughter became another solid and strong creative force in European literature: Mary Shelley,

---

108. Lamott, *Plan B*.
109. Wollstonecraft, "A Vindication of the Rights of Women."

a woman who turned the world of literature upside down with her master-piece, *Frankenstein*.

My point in presenting this example is to say that there are many creative female voices that have been muffled or completely stifled throughout the world, largely because education has not been readily available to them. This wasn't always the case, for Wollstonecraft or Shelley's case (both white women), but it was the case for Harriet Jacobs, the former slave I mentioned earlier, as well as for Edmonia Lewis, a Native American/African American sculptor whose work carried her to Italy as well as to international recognition; and for Billie Holiday, the woman whose plaintive voice set the bar high for jazz/blues vocalists who came after her. Many of the world's cultures celebrated the creative arts with female personae, but it was not easy for any of them.

The Creative Divine

Throughout the world, creativity is primarily represented in the female form. We have the Greek goddesses of the Western world, and the large group of Hindu goddesses in the East, but other smaller civilizations anthropomorphized creativity into a divine feminine.

Aphrodite, the Greek goddess of love and beauty, is considered very creative. She throws herself completely into affairs of the heart or creative projects. She is the muse for dancers, writers, and artists, as I've mentioned before, and though she's no longer worshipped as the goddess of love, she receives a modicum of respect as a muse for the artistic. She's still recognized today in contemporary literature and films, thus it's safe to say that she's a celebrated muse.

In Egyptian mythology, Hathor of Egypt's role is multi-faceted, but for our purposes, I'll stress that she represented music, dance, joy, love, sexuality, and maternal care. She's known as "the Great One of Many Names," and is one of Egypt's most important gods, represented in statuary and paintings as a cow goddess with head horns that hold the sun disk. Human worship of Hathor pre-dates the historical period, so it's hard to tell when it began, but it appears that the people of her time adored her, celebrating the cow goddess with festivals, dances, and songs. In later generations, other cultures adopted this well-known goddess, naming her instead Aphrodite and Venus.

When you speak of creativity in Southeast Asia, everyone refers to Sarasvati, as mentioned previously. Goddess of knowledge and the arts, she usually holds a stringed musical instrument called a veena. Known as "the mother of poetry," it is often stated that she teaches the power of the spoken word and is responsible for every written word.

A major deity in the Hindu religion, Sarasvati is the goddess of wisdom, of the Divine Word (sacred wind). The first major cult to celebrate her was populated by academics and creative people. Today, she is the one who provides a river of inspiration for those who call on her.

Maîtresse Mambo Erzulie Fréda Dahomey, the Haitian Vodou spirit of love, beauty, dancing, luxury, jewelry, and flowers, wears a pink dress, wedding rings, and heart-shaped adornments. She is a spirit who leans more toward eroticism. Her art—dance—reflects the culture of the Western African tribes. Her Catholic image is the Mater Dolorosa.

Benzaiten, a Japanese Buddhist mentioned in the Lotus Sutra, is the patron goddess of literature, music, wealth, and femininity. She's often shown holding a biwa (Japanese lute), similar to Sarasvati and her lute/veena; Benzaiten is often tied to Sarasvati, because of the possibility that she traveled to Japan and may have met Benzaiten.

In Ireland, Brigid (Celtic) is associated with spring, fertility, poetry, and smithcraft. She was often the muse for poets during the Middle Ages, and to this day, Saint Brigid is one of the most recognized figures in Irish history. The primal difference between animal and human are seen in Brigid's culture, as her role as patroness of poetry and spring/fertility intersect. Creativity is born in nature, I believe. Who tells those magnificent birds to wave their purple/orange/fire-engine red feathers in a special dance? How do carpets of lavender cover the largest meadows in perfectly equal rows? The human being takes the creativity nature doesn't think anything of and puts that beauty into a poem or a paintbrush. Brigid defines the role that the arts play in our world.

She is also the keeper of history, the goddess responsible for ensuring that the stories and songs are passed along through generations.

It always surprises me that our various continents, though quite far away from each other, created the same type of beings to worship, particularly when it comes to the arts. People in Africa weren't likely to have spoken to those in Alaska; most of those early civilizations had no idea how to travel to another land—or even if one existed—yet, the goddesses in Africa celebrated dance just as goddesses in Alaska.

For example, Pele, the Hawaiian goddess of fire, is also the goddess of the traditional Hawaiian dance, the hula, yet it was Pele's sister Hi'iaka who was thought to be the first person to actually dance the hula. This cultural dance is not only a movement of the body but is also accompanied by sacred chants that tell epic tales, philosophies, and as a result, preserved history.

My favorite goddesses of the arts are nine minor Greek goddesses called the Muses. Their role in mythology is to personify the arts, and the fact that there are nine of them tells you how important Greece saw the creative arts. In paintings or statuary, the nine are depicted thus: Calliope, usually seen holding a writing tablet, personifies epic poetry. As the "senior muse," she inspired Homer to write the epic poems the *Iliad* and the *Odyssey*. Clio carries a scroll and is protector of history, while Erato, the personification of lyric poetry, carries a cithara (a type of lyre). Poetry was important to the Greeks, so Enterpe is another of the muses, and she represented song and elegiac poetry, carried the aulos (a type of flute), and also created several musical instruments. Melpomene wore a tragic mask and represented tragedy, while Polyhymnia wore a veil over her face and conducted the somber work of personifying hymns. Terpsichore carried a lyre and represented dance, Thalia wore a comic mask to represent her field, and Urania carried a globe and compass to represent astronomy.

The women are the nine daughters of a nine-night union between Zeus and the Titaness Mnemosyne, the goddess of memory. According to myth, they lived on Mount Olympus and entertained the major gods and goddesses who lived there, but it wasn't until the Renaissance that their images were produced in a way to identify them.

The Value of "Women's Arts" and the Ways of Feminine Creativity

One of my interviewees, Kate Stigdon, is an artist, and she describes creativity this way: "I feel much spiritual strength to accomplish and persevere is found in doing inner work and staying creative. I also feel a large part of what motivates me now is my heightened awareness of how women did not really gain the respect and equality that I wanted to believe they attained back in the 1970s and forward. I am now going into my senior years and the retrospective angle becomes keener, finding its way into writing, art, and music. In the past decade, I began using found objects and relics with assemblage techniques in my art. Mixing mediums and honoring the mix relates to the alchemy that life has brought me. Freedom to speak and express/process one's own narrative, encouraging others to as well and listening is important to me. An alternative concept of a 'personal power' model rather than the 'power over' model, in the way I relate is perhaps the most important part of my spiritual awakening process."

I suspect that everyone who's ever planned on sitting at the piano or visiting the studio or putting her fingers on the keyboard would read that statement with fear. No one wants to start over once a project has begun, yet when a book or piece of music or recipe or quilt is pulled apart and begun again, that process teaches us how to analyze our work, use the best we have, and ditch the rest.

Rewriting allows us the opportunity for a do-over, which is basically what Elizabeth Gilbert (author of *Eat, Pray, Love* and a regular Oprah interviewee) is saying. There are many female artists who'd love to have that opportunity.

In art, there's a genre called Outsider Art, a sub-genre of folk art. The work (paintings, sculptures, textiles) is done by untrained artists. It makes sense that women found voices in this genre of art, particularly because a lot of them were not formerly trained. Most of the Outsider Artists come from the South, and their work usually connected to what the artist sees around her neighborhood or home. As with many artists who came before them, these artists usually incorporate materials that are found rather than bought in art supply stores.

These untrained and often unrecognized artists exist all over the world, working in genres ranging from sculpture to murals, paintings, and photography. The fact that these women continue to make art even when faced with major challenges proves how strong the calling is when a person is creative.

One of the lessons we've learned from the art produced by Asian women is that the beauty of simple paintings, calligraphy, and paintings on china is just as fascinating and as much a marker of society during the time it was produced than the formal art produced by educated men during the same period. The art of woodblock prints is one of the best known of the Japanese arts, and Katsushika Oi is one of the most influential artists of the nineteenth century. Even further back in Japanese history, the artist Ike Gyokuran created her paintings during the Edo period and lived in Kyoto. Tenth-century poets decorated their journals with elaborate paintings, literally linking the creative arts.

Finally, let's shine the spotlight on those artists who work in their homes every day and have for centuries: those women who create needlework so fine and delicate that one cannot count the stitches; the female rugmakers who toil for years to create a massive work of art that warms the floor of the house, whether that house's floors are marble or dirt; the women who invented new recipes when the crop failed to survive a frost; the knitters and crotcheters who clothe their families with their hats, blankets, sweaters, and booties; and, last but not least, the women who sing both new and old lullabies and dance babies to sleep with their melodies. Most items created for the home were made by women, but you'll find very few pieces of their homemade works of art in museums around the world.

My Story: Getting Paid

I recently read a study about the salaries of male and female authors, largely for research, but also because I'm always curious whether we female-identifying authors are any better off than female-identifying corporate leaders. I thought that might be changing, largely because so many women writers rule the best-seller lists in their chosen fields.

I was wrong.

The study revealed that not only are titles with obvious male names priced 45 percent higher than those written by women, but also that certain genres have a much lower ratio of women writers to men.[110] It's the same old story: women are paid less than men for the same work. And just like in the distant past, there are some genres where women simply aren't represented.

The study made me sit back in my seat and think for a while. I've seen male friends who write rather lackluster books obtaining interviews with respected book reviewers, like NPR, while their female counterparts with better books have fought for the same privilege and never received it. I think of the authors who are respected by the masses, and the majority of them are male. Yet, when I think of the people who I go to for advice in this business, they are all women. Without exception.

I'm not sure whether it's because men know their worth and demand it, or whether women are simply writing "other things" besides the type of books men are selling. Perhaps the study didn't look at the price difference between hardcover and paperback. That tells us one more thing: are men selling hard-cover books? For the publishers, it's harder to meet rising publishing costs producing hardcover books. With paperbacks, they can sell more and make a better percentage, and since women sell the majority of paperbacks to other women (a recent list by BookBub shows the best book club reads of the past decade; twenty-eight of the books were authored by women, fourteen by men).

My female writer friends and I talk about the types of discrimination in the publishing world, how age has made a difference with my friends who write romances, how the work we're creating is leaning more toward the type of stories men have written for years, and how we've thought about writing under pseudonyms so we'll have the freedom to write what we want. Our writing—our art—has improved through the years of practice. We've learned by teaching others, as we tend to do, and there are some who recognize that

---

110. Flood, "Publishing Industry Is Overwhelmingly White and Female."

women, in general, write and read more than men.[111] Some of my friends even say that if a book they've created is read by the patriarchy, they feel they've finally "made it."

Bullshit.

Those stories written on the kitchen table by women who write about family, love, home life, and relationships are the historical lighthouses that will show future readers what life was like during our time. Women like Jane Austen, the Brontës, Elena Ferrante, Doris Lessing, and Isabel Allende document our lives. Women like P. D. James, Ursula LeGuin, and Octavia E. Butler imagine other worlds and lives. People like Jennifer Finney Boylan, who writes novels as well as *New York Times* columns; Susan Stryker, an American filmmaker, author, and professor; and Jan Morris, a Welsh historian and author, create fiction and nonfiction that is both memorable and important.

I celebrate the feminine in the arts. I hope you embrace your own creativity in any form it takes.

Reflection

Layne Redmond, the author of *When Drummers Were Women*, explored the history of the goddess and the drum in ancient civilizations. As a teacher, historian, and mythologist, Redmond's work is well-respected by musicians, historians, and philosophers. Redmond's work examines how women are turned away from playing the drums, yet they are pictured in early works of art as the ones who held the drum during spiritual and cultural ceremonies.

> *Women need the archetypal image of a Divine Female.*
> *We need to reconnect with the inherent sacredness of*
> *woman as creator and nourisher, rather than accept a*
> *vision of ourselves as less-than-divine inferiors.*[112]
> ~Layne Redmond

---

111. Scholes, "The Female-Only Book Club."
112. Redmond, *When Drummers Were Women.*

In this quote, Redmond encourages women to reconnect with that creative spirit in order to be nourished. Creatives aren't just writers or artists. What do you create? Think about that as you respond. How do you nourish yourself with creativity? You don't have to be a drummer or an artist. One can create in the kitchen or while playing with kids. Be creative in thinking about creativity.

Practice: Keeping a Journal

A journal offers an outlet for creatives as well as those looking for their inner goddess. A blank journal is best, because it leaves room for writing, drawing, ideas, or pinning your favorite blossom. For me, a leatherbound journal invites my comments. I spend at least fifteen minutes each morning writing about the natural elements in the world around me. That truly gives me something new to write about every day, because no day is exactly like the one before it. At other times, I create items out of the seashells I gather every day. I save them on a table in my backyard, and when there are enough, I have a crafts day with one of my friends or one of the children in my family. When I have a finished project, it's incredibly satisfying, and I enjoy the benefits of my labor by using those items in my home.

When you use a journal, you define it the way you want, not the way someone else desires you use it. You can choose a particular topic to write about, if you'd like, or you can leave your inspiration open. You can write one word every once in a while, or you can fill pages every day. You can choose to hide your journal under your mattress, or you can travel the world with it under your arm.

The point is, the journal is yours. Do what you wish and know that it will always be there for you. That's the most important thing to remember: that journal is your place to deliver yourself to its pages.

Main Takeaways from This Chapter

- Defining feminine creativity
- Discussing the goddesses of creativity and the arts
- Valuing the feminine artists

The Goddesses

mara (Scandinavian), female shapeshifters

Frigg (Scandinavian), patroness of the home, Odin's wife

Freyja (Scandinavian), sexually free goddess who practices magic

Inanna (Sumer), goddess of heaven and earth

Lilith (Jewish), seductress, pre-Eve in the Judaic texts

Eve (Christian), first woman on earth

Mary (Christian), mother of Jesus

Ariadne (Greek), Cretan princess in Greek mythology

Chapter Twelve

A Divine Feminine Shell

I often think about author and visionary teacher Sara Wiseman's words that your "body is a divine container that will change over your lifetime." She adds that we should rejoice in those changes, noticing them, and realizing that this "is the way of things: the softening of the shell so the soul can emerge."[113]

I used to talk every couple of days with one of my best friends. She had ALS and her body shut down on her a little more every day, but when we texted, I heard her sarcasm and her cackling laugh through her written words. She always had a way of looking at life with a sense of the irony about it all, and that didn't change, even though she spent her final days creating voice capsules of phrases and sentences she stored for that moment when she would no longer be able to speak.

While she struggled with the end of her life, I continued to conduct research for this book, often finding a quote I'd repeat to her, because it resonated with what she was going through. Sara Wiseman's quote was one we discussed regularly.

My friend's shell of a body wouldn't do the things it used to, wouldn't support her to cross-country ski or to create fanciful crafts as she had for many years prior, even filling her country decorating store on Main Street in Montgomery Center, Vermont. It wouldn't allow her to get out into the garden to smell the perennials she planted there years ago, but her brain still planned and schemed and created. She loved giving me advice on my latest creations, often discussing paint colors and designs with the relish she gave to the artistic work she gave to me and other friends right up until the end.

We spoke about the value of wisdom, and how we had grown with age and were determined to not blow opportunities to do something new like

---

113. Wiseman, SaraWiseman.com.

riding in a helicopter (me) or learning how to paint with watercolors (her). We knew how important it is to make time to play with children or to see an old friend again. We had attained the wisdom to take care of our bodies so they would continue to hold us up during our senior years. We knew that we sometimes didn't take care of our bodies as we should have, because we were intent on mimicking the be-as-skinny-as-you-can trend or covering what we thought were our flaws. Now we know the truth: this shell that we try to make more attractive in order to fit in with everyone else is only that: a shell.

The body holds the mind and the heart, our inner selves, the selves that define us as compassionate and loving or ambitious and powerful. That is most important.

Right before she passed, she sent me one last text: *Live your best life.*

I promised I would.

Early Body Taboos

Many of the world's religions (Christianity, Judaism, Islam, Hinduism, and Buddhism) have restricted menstruating women, leading to prohibitions that range from curtailing physical intimacy to removing the woman from a home where males live).[114]

In cultures all over the world, special menstruation huts are built on the outskirts of a village, where women would be banished during their monthly cycle. The Dogon tribe of Mali have such huts, as well as rules banning sex or dating during the woman's menstruation cycle. On the other side of the world in Indonesia, the Huaulu also banish women to the huts, but they can wander the forests, as long as they stay away from hunters. In the Jewish religion, men and women must refrain from contact during menstruation and for a week afterward. The reason: the menstrual blood, which is the lining of the uterus, is considered unclean.[115]

Christianity also has menstrual taboos similar to other religions, and the menstrual ritual is said to be the reason women don't hold higher positions

---

114. Guterman and Among, *Religions*, 2.
115. Guterman and Among, *Religions*, 2.

in the church. Islam and Hinduism consider the menstruating woman to be "unpure." And while Buddhism calls the cycle "a natural physical exertion that women must go through," there is still an undercurrent of belief that the blood is unclean and that women are likely to lose some of their chi (spiritual energy) during menstruation.[116]

In ancient rituals across the globe, menstruation blood was thought to possess powers that would connect priests and priestesses with the spirits. Some used menstrual blood on crops in order to ensure their fertility. In some cultures, the blood is used to cast spells.

Once the goddess culture started disappearing from ancient religions, the perception that menstruation was dangerous or unclean began softening, though there are still religions that believe in staying away from menstruating females during their cycle. However, women know that the menstrual cycle defines the stages of a woman's life: the first cycle is the passage from girlhood to womanhood, the lack of a menstrual cycle indicates a possible pregnancy in the second stage of the woman's life, and the end of the monthly release of blood from a woman's body also signals her entrance to the last stage of her life: the crone. Though it might have been shocking to some early humans regarding a woman's ability to thrive after bleeding for days, to a woman, those monthly regenerative cycles also allowed her insight to their season of life.

In the Victorian era, it was so shameful for a woman to be pregnant that she spent her time corseted in such a way that it caused permanent changes in the woman's skeleton.[117] Wrapped up tightly, a Victorian woman was not seen as a sexual being, which is what she must have been if she'd become pregnant. The mere thought of the woman having sex was off-putting to them; thus, she had to keep her swelling belly under wraps for as long as possible, and when she started obviously showing, she was kept at home.

Even in today's social circles, a woman might feel it is taboo to discuss her menstrual period, and even in the most forward-thinking companies, a woman might hide her tampons in a brown bag, or discreetly in a pocket or

116. Guterman and Among, *Religions*, 2.
117. Killgrove, "Here's How Corsets Deformed the Skeletons of Victorian Women."

purse. It's definitely not something that's brought up in "polite conversation" or discussed with a man, unless he's a doctor (or a husband).

Women who now embrace the menstrual ritual incorporate it into their monthly routines, celebrating the beauty and sensuality of their own bodies. A woman's womb is powerful, as we know. It is the place where life begins, and there is no greater power than to give birth.

The Fertile and Sensual Goddesses

Most religions celebrate fertility with a female goddess, some of whom also are known for their sensuality and sexual activities. Though some of these sensual creatures are also endowed with negative attributes and can be on the evil side, it is more common for fertility goddesses to be equivalent to those divine feminine beings who recognize and accept their own sexual inclinations.

Scandinavian myths tell stories about women who are shapeshifters who can "disappear quickly, move across great distances in little time, or penetrate walls and locks where no one else can go."[118] Called a *mara*, these female entities were less goddess and more witch, because of their sexual ways, as well as the ability to change shape. People who recognize these beings equate them to night terrors.

Another Scandinavian goddess is Frigg, Odin's wife, who is the patroness of the home and models social virtues for those who appreciate her. A maternal creature, she is known as the Mother Goddess of the North and has maternal qualities, while Freyja, another Scandinavian goddess, is considered a wild woman of the North, because she is sexually free and practices magic. Odin loved Freyja for her beauty. Some theorists believe the two are one woman, while others believe they are two separate goddesses.

In ancient Sumer, Inanna is the most revered deity. A goddess of heaven and earth, Inanna is portrayed as young, radiant, and sexually vibrant, with power over fertility and fecundity of plants, animals, humans. She is the

---

118. Raudvere, *More than Mythology*.

goddess of love and sexual desire and not only flaunts her feminine sexuality, but revels in it.

In other parts of the world, modern women are not like Inanna. They cannot flaunt their sexuality. Interviewee Fizza Imitaz says, "There are several laws applied to only females in our religion: a woman cannot perform Haj alone without her Mehram. [Haj is the annual pilgrimage to Mecca, the holy city, and a Mehram is a member of the family with whom the woman can be unveiled.] She has to stay in her home during *ida'at* (a certain amount of time after being divorced which is three months, or after the death of her husband, which is four months and ten days), to know if she is pregnant or not. And, if she is pregnant, to find a solution that will give her some comfort in her pregnancy. She is also obliged to do hijab and Purdah to cover her head and face." (Hijab is a religious veil worn by Muslim women when they're outside the home, and Purdah is a curtain or clothing that keeps a woman concealed from men and strangers.) In Judaism, Lilith is a woman who appears before Eve in the Talmud. Lilith is often described as a seductress, both evil and frigid. She has no children, though some sources say that she gives birth to as many as one hundred demons a day. Because her role involves both creation and death, she is a complicated divinity.

In *The Divine Feminine: Exploring the Feminine Face of God Around the World,* authors Harvey and Baring bemoan the "tragic Christian tendency to dissociate nature, matter, and the body from divine spirit, because of their association with the 'sin' of Eve is dramatically and finally redeemed in glorious affirmation of their sacredness and divinity." The sin is so entrenched in Christianity that the mother of the Savior, the virginal Mary, was able to give birth without the association of a sexual act.

Though sex is an act that every living thing can experience, it's still viewed by some as sinful for females to flout their sexuality. Instead, the woman who is comfortable with her sexuality and shares the experience as she pleases is often looked upon as a whore. In a recent article in *Psych Alive* about the acceptance of female sexuality, Lisa Firestone, an American psychologist, asks whether women are still being condemned for their sexuality. She states,

"When a person's sexual nature is stripped of these hurtful and shaming cultural and psychological influences, a man and woman's desire for sex is basically the same."[119] If that's the case, one would expect there would no longer be a reason for stating that women who have a healthy sexual appetite are promiscuous.

On the other hand, other religions show the incredible power of women and birth. The story of Ariadne from Greek mythology reminds me of the metaphorical labyrinth, the symbol for the womb, and how the thread that Ariadne lowers to her lover Theseus so that he can escape from the Labyrinth is the equivalent of a mythological umbilical cord. That thread/cord is what ties reality to the otherworld.

Women's Intuition and the Body's Signals

As stated in the beginning of this chapter, every age gives us a new body. Celebrating that new body is difficult for some women to practice, but if you truly believe that it's a gift and that each phase of our body is one to be cherished, that our very existence should be one we relish, and that our relationships to each other, as well as our abilities, are ones we should respect, we should have no problem celebrating our new bodies.

To understand what it means to come to a recognition of yourself as a divine feminine, you must be in touch with your body, recognizing and accepting its abilities. Trust your intuition and when your body signals that something isn't right or might be out of alignment, learn to listen to it and take care of it.

As women, we are used to caring for others, whether we care for children or partners or friends and family. For some reason, our selves come last, when in all actuality, in order to care for others, you must care for yourself first. That might seem selfish at first, but think of it. If you are tired, your chances of offering loved ones the care you want to give them is diminished.

---

119. Firestone, "Are We Still Condemning Women for their Sexuality?"

If you are sick, how can you adequately minister to others who are also ill? If you have emotional trauma in your life, how can you help others to heal?

Many mind-body therapists remind us to be loving of our own bodies and minds, and they encourage healthy eating, deep sleep, yoga or exercise, meditation, nature walks, and self-kindness. When we honor the body and mind for which we are the sole caretakers, we open ourselves up to being invested in our own wellness and that, in itself, opens the channels for our inner voice to revel in silence or reverence for the sacred. It also can open us up to the natural intuitions we have but are taught to ignore.

Elizabeth Gilbert believes that "we overthink things. Partially in my life as a writer, I've really learned to trust my instincts about the projects that I'm working on, and to go towards something, even though it doesn't make sense, because I feel like I want to know more about that."[120] Personally, trusting my instincts has been one of the hardest things for me to learn. I'm always questioning whether I'm making the right choice, whether in my career projects or in my personal relationships. I believe a lot of us feel the same way, and learning how to accept and trust your instinct is something that takes time and trust.

Surprisingly, our time at the bottom of the ladder has taught us well how to recognize body clues and facial expressions, largely enabling us to have that "women's intuition" everyone talks about.

If your gut feeling is something you tend to ignore, even though there are times you can look back on an incident and realize that your instincts had been right, there's still time to pay attention to your intuition. Sit with yourself and find those goddesses you feel connected to and call on them to give you the strength to trust yourself.

Body Image

Years of non-acceptance creates body shame, negative or hurtful thoughts about the body and the self. Most women I know refer to themselves and

---

120. Gilbert, *Big Magic*.

their bodies negatively. They buy into the belief that women must be A+B to equal the C that is acceptable. Fill in those A+B factors with whatever you believe, and then throw out that belief and replace it with a new one. Know that you are perfect exactly the way you are.

For many, it's a huge step to accept their bodies as perfect just the way they are, learning to celebrate full-hipped women, full bodies, as goddesses, sensual, not threatening. In the past, voluptuosity has equated with wealth and women who had lush bodies were admired. It's only during the last hundred years that thinness has been desirable. But that doesn't mean it's right for everyone. Each body is different, as is each person. As long as you're celebrating who you are and what type of body you have, you will embody the beautiful spirit inside of you.

Someone once said that the more she studied animals, the better she understood human beings. I understand what she means. We believe we are the most civilized species, yet we do not recognize that it's natural for the females of the species to preen and shake their tail feathers like a peacock. Though, as a society, we have struggled with recognizing and stopping body shaming, we still have much to learn. Here's where the narrative changes.

None of the goddesses mentioned in this book wear their bodies and the clothes that cover them with a sense of shame. They are who they are— undersea goddesses, goddesses of war, women who lived their lives looking out rather than judging themselves. Instead, the divine feminine celebrates the strengths they have without wasting time comparing themselves to someone else.

One of my interviewees, Meenu Akbar Ali, says that she thinks "celebrating femininity may break the patterns in toxic masculinity and patriarchal attitudes. It should also help the LGBTQ+ community." Perhaps she has a point that by accepting and loving our own feminine bodies, we might encourage the patriarchy to respect our selves, as well. If that happens, could you give off an aura that will automatically encourage others to respect us, as well?

That animalistic instinct to attract becomes complicated when you add a human being's ability to reason and think logically. We begin to impose impossible expectations on ourselves and each other, unable or unwilling to accept people as they are without meeting society's rules for what constitutes attractiveness.

What most people don't talk about is how ageist we are toward older women.

Most women over sixty deal with an aging body. Her bones aren't as strong, her coloring is fading, her skin wears the wrinkles of too many smiles—or frowns. Why is that a negative in our culture? Here's the truth for most of us: those wrinkles are the sign of a life well-lived, and she is still strong, she can out-hike her daughter who sits behind a desk twelve hours a day, and that older woman is supple, especially after her Tuesday/Thursday afternoon yoga class. She worked her way up in the company (school/hospital/creative art) and is now looking at what her second (or third) act will be. She's smart, loves traveling (sometimes with her grandkids or to visit them, sometimes by herself, exploring the world she hasn't yet had a chance to visit). She's learned a lot through the years, and her untapped well of information is valuable. She's that wise crone we talked about earlier.

But society has checked out on anyone who might be less than vibrant or able to successfully hide any vestige of having spent a long time experiencing life. The advertising world tells women of a certain age to have their photos touched up if a vein shows in a leg or a wrinkle creases below the left eye. Cosmetic companies sell women creams and lotions to cover their crepey skin or liver spots, believing that those badges of honor for life lived with zest is not a badge of honor at all. Some people recoil at the sight of a woman's knobby hand, instead of marveling at the thousands of days those hands spent over a keyboard sending missives to lawyers and politicians, editors and daughters, friends and soon-to-be-friends. Lovers. Children.

I call bullshit, and I hope you do, too, especially for our sisters who cannot do so.

In some countries, females live under strict rule. Maria Farooq Maan, one of my interviewees, says, "Are there rules of laws applied only to the females in my religion? If I answer this question by only telling what rules are only applied to females, I will be overlooking rules which are only applied to males and will be at the risk of adding to the narrative that sees the two as binaries.

So it is only when things are looked at holistically that you see the set of certain rules is the safeguarding of others' rights." Those rules often state what a woman can wear, whether she should cover her hair, where she lives while going through her menstrual cycle. When the patriarchal society has control over a female's physical appearance, that society controls a woman's vision of herself.

Instead of valuing women as they grow older, most of our world tends to turn their backs. The crone's bastion of wisdom isn't valued. They are told what not to wear. They read articles about the "Ten Best Hairstyles for Women Over Fifty." They are advised not to post pics of themselves that show the rich life they led raising their own kids (and sometimes their sister's or their children's kids or kids who belong to neighborhood families). They hide those beautiful arthritic hands they earned from doing piecework at the factory for years. They use dark glasses to disguise the deep wrinkles that make their knowing eyes disappear when they laugh (which is often, by the way). They wear long skirts because seniors shouldn't show their knees. In other words, their bodies and value to society are shamed instead of elevated and appreciated. We should celebrate those who are venerable instead of believing that because a mind or a body is aged, it is no longer valuable. That is simply not the truth.

Not only are women hyper-aware of their bodies, but some of us compete against each other as the goddesses would on a grander scale. We women are often our own worst enemies when it comes to being ageist. Having experience born of years should be an enviable place to be, to have lived long enough to gain some wisdom simply because of life experiences. That wisdom has nothing to do with the type of job you have or the money you've earned or the status you've achieved. Life wisdom comes through heartbreak and happiness. It comes from birth and death, from pleasures and pain. A balanced life.

One of the best things to come from the Baby Boomer era is that people learned how to fight for what they wanted. Aging American women have begun to follow earlier European examples where women build communities for themselves, based on their needs and philosophical bent. Women discovered that as they aged they weren't ready to live in a home or with family members. They had no real need for someone else's money or physical strength. They wanted community, and they found it with people like them, often other women

All animals divide themselves, whether it's into flocks or gaggles, clans or herds, murders or congresses. Women who build their own communities have figured that out and found their own bevy of friends/family/chosen family who share the same philosophy. Since those early experimental communities, other groups of women have founded their own version of a home-community where everyone contributes somehow to the betterment of the whole. It's a win-win situation that allows women the independence and self-sufficient lifestyle they desire.

My Story: Grieving the Mother

When my mother passed away, I felt more bereft than I'd ever felt before. She wasn't the first person I'd lost. My grandparents, whom I was close to, were already gone. I'd lost two cousins before making it to my teens, and one of my best friends died when I was in my early twenties (I still can't talk about her without crying). But my mother was the person I called every day for advice, the one I could count on to be honest with me, and the one I knew loved me unconditionally, even when I was being a little shit (and I was, on occasion!). She understood me in ways my father never could; she understood me as a woman.

My husband tried to console me, but he failed. Somehow, he expected me to get past the grief within the first week. That wasn't going to happen, and he didn't understand that until he lost his own mother years later. My family had their own grief to contend with; we all had different relationships with my mother, and as a result, a different type of grieving to do.

A week after I returned to my teaching position, I was driving to the college to assist in registering new students for classes when a song came on the radio that my mother used to sing to us when we were little. I barely made it to the school, and when I did, I sought my best friend, taking her outside under a live oak tree, where I dissolved in tears.

But my grieving wasn't done. I swallowed my tears that day, knowing that I had work to do, and that the people I worked with figured I'd had my bereavement days. It was time to move on.

A month later, in my yoga class, I lay on the floor in *savasana*, deep into my lying meditation, and suddenly, my whole body shook uncontrollably though I had the solid floor of the gym beneath me. Behind my eyelids, I envisioned a purple flash, as though I'd entered another level of meditation. But I think something truly broke inside me that day, a level of grief that brought me to a deep understanding of what our bodies hold tight inside.

It was a grief that became a release from deep within, from the very core of who I am. Tears rolled down my face, and I let them, still lying in *savasana*, still surrendering myself to the floor beneath me, still trusting that the earth would support me. The quakes within me released, each one like the lock in a dam that allows a certain flow of water through, then stops. I felt the tightness in my belly loosen, then the sadness lifted from my chest, and my shoulders released. Still, the silent tears flowed down my face.

When I finally opened my eyes, everyone else was gone except for my yoga instructor, who'd also become a dear friend. She knew I'd been struggling with losing my mother and let me experience the release of grief while she remained seated in her own meditation pose. I felt like I'd been held in a loving embrace.

It was then that I realized the power of one woman to help another: the power we all have to help and give solace.

Reflection

Robin Rumi is a writer and educator who has spent the past couple of decades studying various philosophical experiences. In this quote, she reminds us that we're all a mirror image of those divine women discussed throughout this book.

All women are a reflection, a mirror of the Goddess.
Remember … you are the Universe figuring itself out. So, of
course, you are identical to the female aspect of divinity.[121]
~Robin Rumi

To be aware of your own mirror image and to see that reflection as holy or divine doesn't mean you have to be conceited or that you're creating an idolatrous image. Noticing that you (and the Universe within you) are figuring yourself out is a good thing. I believe we should constantly be working toward a better understanding of ourselves. If we don't understand ourselves, how can anyone else? How are you recognizing your own image? Replace any negativity with the polar opposite: the positive. What is it about you that makes you special?

More Suggested Practices

- Celebrate the natural occurrences of your body.
- Howl at the moon on the eve of your cycle.
- Dig your toes in the sand during the Summer Solstice.
- Join the Red Hat Society once you're "of age."
- Accept every change in your body and every era of your life that gives you a new body to enjoy.

Main Takeaways from This Chapter

- Considering the value of wisdom
- Banishing the female body
- Learning about the goddesses of fertility
- Listening to the body's signals
- Grieving our mothers

---

121. Rumi, "Writing about Spirituality, Love and Connection."

The Goddesses

Inanna (Sumerian), goddess of heaven and earth

Lilith (Jewish), early biblical figure (pre-Eve)

Eve (Biblical), first woman (in Judaism, Eve is the second female, after Lilith)

Virgin Mary (Christian), mother of Jesus

Ariadne (Greek), Cretan princess associated with mazes and labyrinths

Andal/Kothai (Hindu), one of the twelve devotional saints called Alvars

Chapter Thirteen

The Divine Spiritual Journey

Though our religious beliefs differ, we might not share the same traditions or culture, and we might not even share a common language, I do believe we all share a spiritual journey of some sort, and more commonalities than differences.

One of my interviewees, Naqeeba Zafar says: "Divine or sainted ones are considered to be extraordinary beings, who possess outstanding spiritual and intellectual powers. Divine beings have nothing to do with lustful desires and worldly pleasures that an ordinary human being seems to enjoy. Moreover, they are compassionate and benevolent towards mankind."

We know now that, starting with the original Earth Mother, all religions mention divine women, some too briefly, but in all, women are the original archetypes (e.g., Mary Magdalene, Kwan Yin, Isis, Tara). We understand that certain personality traits have been attributed to the feminine, and we celebrate those qualities. We embrace the connections our goddesses had to the land and the living beings with which we share it.

The biggest question, to me, is why we are judged if we want to celebrate the divine feminine? Often if a woman states that she is celebrating the phases of the moon or is aligning herself with a certain goddess, she is given the side eye or a raised eyebrow. If we smudge our homes or brew a restorative tea, some believe that we are strange. Why? Celebrating the divine feminine doesn't mean replacing the divine masculine. On the contrary, it simply means including the feminine divinity/goddess/face of god with the same type of pomp and circumstance we afford other gods. And it means celebrating the feminine self with all the respect due any divine female.

It is assumed that in early herding times, the Neolithic period, when early humans became hunter-gatherers, men converted some of the earliest gods from female to male, then the male icon took over. However, anthropologists and archeologists have uncovered some early villages (occupied approximately 9,000 years ago) and pottery figures of female goddesses are commonly found. Some of them are called "Venuses," because the figures celebrate the feminine figure.[122] Go to any museum that celebrates archeology and you'll find an example.

During the digs, archeologists find evidence of seeds, a sign that the people of the area were moving from being hunter-gatherers to farmers. Women were largely responsible for sowing and growing, at that time, while the men hunted, fished, gathered, and protected.

Combine that natural movement of evolution as people learn to live and thrive in their environment, with the phenomenon of henotheism (where the hierarchy of gods adjusts so that the qualities of two or more gods are combined, creating one god where there once was more), and you have one plausible reason why the number of feminine deities began to shrink.

Through the years to come, the lack of those goddesses impacted each of the geographical regions where the phenomenon occurred, and the change often resulted in the very opposite of the adoration goddesses had previously been afforded. Often, the culture reacted, punishing those who wanted to continue worshipping the goddess and degrading the human beings who resembled her: women.

The Divine Journey, Part 2

Each of the women I've spoken with during my research (and for years before I started this book!) has had a full and interesting spiritual journey. The pieces of these stories weave together showing us that all of our spiritual journeys are linked, a long line of inspirational stories that highlight the underlying modesty and quiet strength of every woman I've known. Whether

---

122. Female Figure, Egyptian, Brooklyn Museum, https://www.brooklynmuseum.org/opencollection/objects/4225.

a woman is highly devoted to her belief system or has chosen not to attach herself any kind of religion or philosophy, there's a story about her journey that started many, many years before she was born. I believe that our journey started after the hunter-gatherer period when the goddesses took the back seat and human women went with them.

Who are the feminine divinities who paved the way with their own interesting journeys?

In the ninth century, the Hindu saint known as Andal (the only woman among the twelve devotional saints called Alvars) began her life as the foster child of Saint Periyalvar. A childless man, he found Andal under a Tulasi plant and took her in, giving her a life filled with poetry and devotion. He and his wife named her Kothai (gift of Mother Earth), and she became a devotee of Lord Krishna.

Andal's image shows a young woman with large, dark eyes and a friendly smile. She is draped with a colorful garland of flowers to symbolize the ones she dedicated to Vishnu. Afterward, she received her name, Andal, and the nickname Chudikodutha Sudarkodi, which means "the lady who gave her garland to Vishnu."

Andal's story—from orphaned child, to favored foster child, to honored saint—seems more the story of a motivated and blessed human being, but she has many of the divine feminine qualities mentioned throughout any text on the subject. Her journey took her to the very heart of her own faith, and as a result of her devotion, she, too, is worshipped.

Some divine feminine human beings are not as likely to cultivate a following.

In Sri Lanka, an order of fully ordained nuns existed for more than a thousand years. The order was devastated when an invading Hindu force cast women in a lower status than men, destroying a millennium of history and a veneration of the divine feminine in a matter of days.

Until the time when invaders from Greece, Rome, and other cultures swarmed through northern Africa, "[t]he goddesses in Egypt were the Tree of Life—the date palm and the sycamore tree with its milky sap—and were often shown as the tree, offering from its leafy interior vases that contained the water of eternal life, nourishment for the souls passing from one dimension to another."[123] Ironically, some of the goddesses are still celebrated, but not in Egypt. The religion of ancient Egypt somehow migrated to southern and central Africa.

It's only recently that women have been able to preach from most pulpits or to have any kind of administrative roles in most churches. *Christianity Today*[124] states that one out of every eleven pastors is female. *ChurchTimesUK* states that more women than men are currently entering clergy training.[125] In 2006, Kathrine Jefferts Schori became the first female Presiding Bishop in the history of the Episcopal church, yet as recently as 2008, Jackie Roese had to have a bodyguard when delivering her first sermon at Irving Bible Church near Dallas, Texas.[126] If your spiritual journey brings you to your chosen religion and your motivation is to reach the highest pinnacle, you have more of a chance now than for the past millennium. Take it!

My Story: My Prayer Ritual

I spoke earlier about my own spiritual journey and how I came to Buddhism, but now that I'm at the end of this book, I'd like to talk about the altar in my room.

When I was growing up and going to church all the time, I treasured the moments I could stand in front of the altar in the vestry and simply admire the rich simplicity of it. I wanted more than anything to be an acolyte, to light those candles, and on the rare occasion when I could, I felt the sacredness of that tradition more deeply than I've felt anything else.

I feel a little of that holy ritual every time I light a candle in my home (and I have at least one lit at most hours of the day). I usually send a little prayer

123. Harvey and Baring, *The Divine Feminine.*
124. *Christianity Today,* "50 Women You Should Know."
125. Williams, "More Women Than Men Enter Clergy Training, Latest Figures Show."
126. Evans, *A Year of Biblical Womanhood.*

up to my mother or my grandmother or a little "wish on a star" to help me through the day. I do the same thing as I blow them out.

I knew, when it was time for me to get my own altar for my Buddhist practice, that I wanted something as simple and beautiful as the altar in that Methodist church where I'd grown up. I wanted the altar to reflect the bridge between my belief systems. The one thing that felt odd—not uncomfortable or mysterious, but unknown—was the rich golds and brilliant reds and bright yellows of the altars some of my Buddhist friends had in their homes. They seemed too much to me. A bit over the top.

I hunted for a month, looking at altars (in this case, it's a type of box that holds the scroll for my Buddhist sect, Soka Gakkai), and I found some simple black ebony choices, a few made of teak, and some made of elaborate plastic. Finally, I found the one I wanted: a simple, blond pine with no accoutrements whatsoever.

It was perfect.

Buddhist altars hold pieces that represent mind, spirit, and body: the elements of the human being that we focus on while trying to achieve enlightenment. Choosing items to install once my altar was properly placed (unless you don't have space, it shouldn't be in a bedroom) and at the proper height (above your head when you are meditating) was easy. I had a statue of Buddha that felt right to me, an incense holder, a shallow bowl, a small meditation gong, and a few books, all of which fit nicely on the small bookcase that held my altar.

My mentor came to my house the day we installed my Gohonzon (sacred scroll) inside the box. He taught me how to care for it, we conducted a small ceremony, and he left.

I sat for a long time, staring at the Gohonzon, praying a little, thinking about my ancestors and how weird they probably would think I was. I found a strange comfort in their imagined discomfort. I had come a long way between what my parents and grandparents believed and what finally felt right to me. I had questioned my Methodist upbringing, had explored Catholicism, studied with Jehovah's Witnesses, asked a lot of questions of Mormons, and spent some time not believing anything at all. My choice of religion was my choice, and it felt right. The gift of exploring and finding what feels right to you is something I wish for everyone.

Sitting in my meditation room that day, I knew I'd keep studying, and I have, and I knew I'd always maintain an open ear to listen to the stories of how others found their belief system. Diving deep into the divine feminine is a necessary rite of passage for me.

Namaste.

Reflection

Luisah Teish is an Iyanifa and Oshun chief in the Yoruba tradition. She is the author of several books about celebrations and traditions, as well as articles in magazines such as *Essence* and *The Yoga Journal*. Her published works include *Jambalaya: The Natural Woman's Book of Personal Charms and Practical Rituals*.

> *Oya-Yansa is the Queen of the Winds of change. She is feared by many people because she brings about sudden structural change in people and things. Oya does not just rearrange the furniture in the house, she knocks the building to the ground and blows away the floor tiles.*[127]
> ~Luisah Teish

A goddess who has the power to "knock the building to the ground and blow away the floor tiles" is quite the decorator. That natural element of having the power to control the winds is typical of the divine feminine. But let's think about the winds of change as a spiritual metaphor. What kind of change have you brought to your own life or the lives around you? Are you ready to make or break traditions? Can you make a plan for that?

---

127. Teish, *On Holy Ground*.

Practice: Spiritual Rituals

All religions celebrate small rituals or traditions by praying or practicing their beliefs in a specific-to-that-spirituality way. Even if you don't recognize them as spiritual rituals, per se, women practice the same traditions that churches, temples, synagogues, mosques, and chapels do. When we light candles, practice yoga or meditation, create a prayer circle, cook healing foods, comfort a friend with a contemplation, or create a space for the sacred, divine guides, ancestors, or angels, we are practicing the types of rituals that have been used to invoke the spirit for centuries—millennia, actually.

Sometimes the simple act of lighting a candle is enough to bring peace to your soul. So, here's what your practice is for today:

Find a candle whose scent appeals to you, and when you light it, breathe in that aroma. Take three deep inhales and exhales. By the third one, you should feel that aromatherapy settling into your body. Close your eyes and repeat a prayer you know. If you don't know one, repeat this simple mantra I hear all the time during yoga practice: "I am enough, I do enough, I am exactly where I need to be."

As you whisper that prayer, place your hands over your heart space and feel that powerful organ beating beneath your fingertips.

You are not only enough, you are divine. Remember that.

Main Takeaways from This Chapter

- Examining the role of women in religion
- Appreciating the spiritual journey of all women
- Knowing You are Divine

Chapter Fourteen

A Plan for Being Divine

Now that you've come to the end of this book, hopefully you connected with one of the dozens of divine feminine we've discussed, one who speaks to you and with whom you might identify. Or you recognize strengths—like cultivating relationships, caring for the earth, or leading a company—that you might share with a goddess you'd never heard of before. If you connect with Athena but you're of another faith, that doesn't mean you have to take a sharp turn off your original spiritual journey. All it means is that you can recognize some of those goddess qualities also exist in you.

That's the point, isn't it? If we look to those we emulated for centuries, we can discover that those goddesses are all simply exaggerated versions of us. Yes, us. We are more than a goddess who specializes in only one area. We are Athena's wisdom plus Sarasvati's artistic talents and Mary's patience and Diana's clear-thinking. We are not just one divine feminine; we are all of them. All of creation exists in all of us.

If one thing reverberates for you as a result of reading this book, I hope it is that you deserve the same respect, adoration, love, dedication, admiration, and devotion that you would give to any deity, no matter your religion.

I believe that by recognizing yourself as divine, you will act that way toward others, and you will not accept anything less than the respect and love you deserve. You are worthy of recognition for simply being who you are. If we see that about ourselves, we'll also notice that in all things.

I would go on making my pitch for the perfect, peaceful, compassionate society, but I'm not looking to change the world here. I want you to do that. You can do that.

You can.

Practice: Connecting with the Goddess

Choose one of the divine feminine you've met on these pages (the list at the beginning of each chapter should help you) and concentrate on the qualities that draw you to them. Is it Diana's connection with animals or Joan of Arc's unwavering support of her country? Do you feel like Mother Nature because of the sense of peace and happiness you find in the garden? Sit quietly, whether someplace inside or outside, where others will leave you alone. Concentrate on the image you have of the divinity you have chosen. Think about the aspects of her personality that resonate with you. Sit with those images until you have at least qualities of hers that match with qualities of your own character. Remind yourself of those qualities. Repeat each three times to yourself. See yourself embodying those qualities. When you finish with your meditation, write those qualities on a piece of paper and put the note away. (Someday, when you find that note, you will be reminded of those qualities that I suspect you're already embodying.)

Practice: Recognizing Yourself as Divine

During the next week, start each day with a mirror affirmation. Look at yourself, lift that beautiful chin of yours, and say: "I am divine, you are divine, I respect you, you respect me." Throughout the day, repeat this mantra silently to yourself and be aware of the ways you respond to those with whom you come into contact. Be careful to be kind to yourself. If you recognize someone treating you with disrespect, respond kindly and compassionately to them, asking for the respect you deserved. In addition, if you act disrespectfully to someone, recognize that, forgive yourself, and move on, reminding yourself to act respectfully toward the next person you meet. Finally, end the evening with another mirror affirmation, repeating the one that started your day. If you practice this for an entire week, it should become a natural habit, reminding you of your own divinity and that you share that divine nature with others on the earth, as well.

Moving Forward

One of the things that became clear from the most recent upsurge in feminism (call it the #metoo movement or persistence or women in government) is that it is time to recognize our own role in ruling the world in which we live. Sometimes that's not always going to be an easy pill to swallow. For thousands of years, we've been taught by society to stay in our places, whatever that might mean for the individual. We've gotten so good at it that we've forgotten how to claim the respect we're due. But I believe it's happening. We're raising a voice. A unified voice.

Here are some thoughts I have about the challenges we might face because we're still fighting that inequality in the workplace, as well as in government. Though we've made great strides, there are still plenty of glass ceilings left to break through.

If you want to succeed in industry of any kind, and you've never been part of a team, get on one now. Make sure your children all join teams. They don't have to be physical sports teams, but instead teams that rely on the individual talent each brings to the team as a whole. You need to work as a team in industry. So, instead of competing against other women, learn how to support each other, and how to work as a team. Find your fellow goddesses. There is nothing we cannot do when we link arms!

In your relationships, it's more important than ever to consider carefully the type of reaction your actions might invite. Respect starts with you, but you also need to cultivate the ability to think about how your actions might hurt another divine feminine. Respect everyone. If women respect women, it is only a matter of time before everyone else falls into line.

It's funny how your perspective changes as you move through different eras in your life. In her memoir, Anne Lamott bemoans the early years of the war in Iraq and the Bush presidency. Though I lived through those years and discussed it every day with my colleagues, a lot of proverbial water has gone under the bridge since then. When I remember the daily death statistics from the coronavirus during 2020/2021, nothing could have been worse.

I think of seeing those years from some point in the future, looking back at old photographs, reading the pieces I wrote, seeing the old news reports, and I realize that, in the future, I will look younger, the news will be history instead of current events, that anything that has happened since then determines how I might have looked at the event on that particular day—but it doesn't reflect the wisdom I might have accumulated since then. I might have been worried about a couple of extra pounds around my middle or the way the person taking the photo had just spoke to me, or whether I'd be able to meet a deadline or see a friend. All the thoughts we currently consider necessary to act upon will feather into the atmosphere like the ghost of a dove. I won't remember one thought from that past, any more than I know what my thoughts will be like only five minutes into the future.

Knowing that fact makes it no easier to understand, but it certainly does make one thing crystal clear: that photo I find to be unflattering now will look pretty damn good twenty years from now. It's just another reminder that perspective changes everything.

Try to imagine today what your perspective of your current situation will be five years from now. Does it change things for you?

How to Implement the Divine Feminine into Daily Life

How much you celebrate your inner divine feminine is, of course, up to you. You'll find your own rituals and traditions that feel right for you. I encourage you to build them for yourself and to celebrate them alone. I have several I do during different seasons of the year, and when I complete them, my world feels both brighter and more peaceful.

Final Practices: You Are Divine

Though there are practices offered throughout this book, here are some that might fit into your daily routine.

- Relish the first moments when you first open your eyes. Notice your surroundings. Listen to the sounds outside your bedroom space. Take a good deep breath and let that breath flow through your whole body. Unclench your jaw. Stretch. Let your body feel the gentle silence that leaves within moments after awakening. Find pleasure in those moments. Put your feet on the floor and know the earth—Mother Nature—supports you.

- Honor your sacred space. Create a place where you can connect with the spiritual being inside you. Keep items there (e.g., photos of your ancestors, candles, natural elements, pictures or statues of divine beings who resonate with you) that will remind you of your own divine feminine. Connect with those photos whenever you want to send a special prayer into the universe.

- Elizabeth Gilbert, author of the bestselling *Eat, Pray, Love*, has "a chanting book of my favorite prayers," and whenever she's away from home she chants the prayers, practices meditation, and knows she's "home."[128] Owning a book like that (or, better yet, creating one yourself) can give you an anchor when you're not in your own space. Carry it (or something like it) whenever you'll be in need of the sweetness of your home and/or family.

- Sometimes a ritual can be as simple as a bubble bath. As you prepare your space, think about the divine feminine with whom you connect. What is it about her that you would like to honor? Gather a white candle, your bubbles, and your favorite beverage (something sparkling would be wonderful). Fill your tub with water, empty your bubble bath into the water, and light your candle. Turn off the lights and stand for a moment in the silence. Smell the candle's scent. Feel the floor beneath

---

128. Noda, "Authors in Conversation."

your feet, the air on your body. Place your candle next to the tub and climb in. As you sink beneath the bubbles, think about the divinity you admire and say her name aloud. Ask for her support or guidance, giving her the full respect she deserves. Pour a bit of your bubbly into the bath, as a gift to your goddess and to yourself. When you let the tub drain, thank your divinity for joining you.[129]

- Remind yourself at least once a day of the divine feminine virtues you embody, and include in that reminder an assurance that these virtues are valuable and necessary in today's world. Pass along that same type of reminder to any other divine feminine you come into contact with throughout your day. Nothing feels better than to make eye contact and to smile at a woman who's been on her feet behind the counter since she dropped her kids at school five hours before. Let someone else know you see them.

- Listen to music every day. Support local musicians, galleries, theater, and dancers with your presence. Go to free library events or coffee-houses and listen to poets. Feed your Sarasvati soul!

- If you cook a bit extra, share it with someone else. If you have time to spare, spend it with a person who has no family. If you care about an issue in your neighborhood, town, or state, volunteer to help. Whenever you give, you are certain to receive something in return, even if it's simply a heartfelt thank you.

- Pay it forward! Do it in the fast-food line or at a grocery store. It doesn't have to be a lot.

- Conduct your business with an eye toward doing no harm. Create a safe place for everyone with whom you work. Assume that safe space for yourself, as well.

- Visit someone else's place of worship. Watch the women. Learn about their roles. Ask about their traditions. Listen.

---

129. Inspired by James Duvalier.

- Volunteer—for anything! Read books to folks in nursing homes. Teach someone how to read. Coach a little league team. Give out food at the homeless shelter.

- If you want to fly a helicopter, find a way to do it. Maybe you just want to make yourself a vegetable garden or you'd love to grow roses. Do it. If you have a passion for learning other languages, check out the local library for CDs or find a partner and learn together. Just make "do it" part of your vocabulary.

- Talk to someone you love, heartfelt and earnestly. Touch the person when you speak to her/him. Make eye contact. Say how you feel.

Celebrating the Feminine: Exploring Further

We've shared dozens of stories about goddesses. I'm sure that one or more has spoken to you. Explore more! Doors to women's worlds that you may not have been privy to before are now open to you: the world of nuns—both Catholic and otherwise; the female deities from all over the world; the saints and witches and women with incredible healing powers; women who've been part of every religion and philosophy ever created.

It's amazing to read or hear their stories and to recognize what they brought to a culture or a people. And, conversely, what a loss it would be to the very fabric of a region if those stories were blotted out forever—or never added to or embroidered upon for future generations. My voice is not the only one out there, nor is my view of the divine feminine the only one. There are as many versions as there are world religions.

I'm sure one of these divine women has spoken to you. Keep your mind open, learn all you can, and remember to honor the divine in yourself.

Glossary

Deity: a goddess (or god) who is worshipped by people of faith, or who is recognized as a supreme being.

Devi: the supreme female goddess in the Hindu religion; the goddess who transcends immortality and infuses other goddesses with the ability to be a heavenly being.

Dharmshala: a sanctuary or sacred dwelling.

Divine: a goddess or heavenly being; or being like a goddess or heavenly being.

Divine feminine: a being embodying the best qualities of a feminine being: the balance of earth-like connections with mystical; the complete acceptance and honoring of all elements that are considered female. The divine feminine works for the good of all people, raises up the level of compassion for all beings, is the protector and the giver of life, is the embodiment of love and understanding, serves light instead of greed, chooses to serve instead of exploit, and celebrates the sacredness of all life.

Ecofeminism: a belief that the ecology of the world and the suppression of feminine strength are connected.

Feminine: any person who identifies as female.

Goddess: a female deity or a person who resembles a female deity in actions and temperament.

Goddess consciousness: a state of being that is connected to the divine feminine self (though one does not need to be gender specific). It is an "elevated, ego-diminished, non-judgmental and non-harming state of being" (Bashford).

Mirror stage: Labeled by the philosopher Jacques Lacan, it is the stage in psychoanalytic development when an infant sees its own image for the first time and begins to place him/herself in the world around him/her.

Sacred: connected to goddesses/deities or to religion; calls for veneration and respect; the sacred gives birth and celebrates it.

Theology: the study of religion, especially where a deity is involved.

Theosophy: a philosophy based on the mystical insight into the nature of the Goddess (or God) and the Universe.

Full List of the Goddesses

Allat (Arabic), fertility goddess

Amaterasu (Shinto), sun goddess

Andal/Kothai (Hindu), one of the twelve devotional saints called Alvars

Annapurna (Hindu), mountain goddess

Aphrodite (Greek), goddess of love, beauty, creativity, and passion

Ariadne (Greek), Cretan princess associated with mazes and labyrinths

Artemis/Diana (Greek/Roman), goddess of wild animals and the hunt

Athena (Greek), goddess of war and education

Auset (Egyptian), mother goddess of crops, magic, and personal spirituality

Awitelin Tsita (Native American), earth mother

Baba Yaga (Russian), Mother Earth witch

Bathsheba (Christian), biblical mother of Solomon

Berizaiten (Japanese Buddhist), patron goddess of literature, music, wealth, and femininity

Bhagavati (Hindu) or Devi, the female aspect of Shakti (divine masculine), power beyond the universe

Brigid (Celtic), goddess of spring, fertility, poetry, and smithcraft

Brigid (Irish), mother of Irish gods

Calliope (Greek), goddess of epic poetry

Candaces/Kentakes (Kushite), warrior queens

Ceridwen (Welsh Celtic), goddess of prosperity

Ch'ang O (Chinese), moon goddess

Cleopatra (Egyptian), queen celebrated as both human and divine

Clio (Greek), goddess protector of history

Cybele (ancient Phrygia), goddess of fertility and protectress in time of war

Damona (Gallo-Roman), goddess of wealth and fertility

Deborah (Christian), led the army of Israel via commands from God

Deer Woman (Plains), associated with love and fertility

Deidre (Irish), legendary figure promised to royalty but in love with another

Demeter (Greek), goddess of the grain

Dhat-Badan (Arabic), goddess of natural forces of the wilderness

Diana/Artemis (Roman/Greek), goddess of the hunt and domesticated animals, moon goddess and protector of newborns

Durga (Hindu), goddess of war, strength, and protection

Earth Woman (Okanagan), mother of everyone

Enterpe (Greek), goddess of song and elegiac poetry

Erato (Greek), goddess personification of lyric history

Esther (Jewish), biblical queen married to Persian King Xerxes I; saved the Jewish nation by interceding

Eve (Biblical), first woman (in Judaism, Eve is the second female, after Lilith)

Fatima (Arabic), moon goddess

Fox Woman (Cree/Ojibwe), wise elder spirit

Gaia (Greek), personification of the earth

Grandmother Woodchuck (Abenaki), wise old woman who raises a hero

Hagar (Jewish), handmaiden to Sara

Harriet Jacobs (African American), activist for slave education

Hathor (Egyptian), goddess of music, dance, joy, love, sexuality, and maternal care

Hera (Roman), goddess of marriage and fertility

Hestia (Greek), goddess of the hearth

Inanna (Sumerian), goddess of heaven and earth; goddess of war

Inanna/Ishtar (Egyptian/Babylonian), goddess of sensuality and warfare, goddess for animals and everything that grows

Isis (Egyptian), cosmic mother, goddess of love, fertility, resurrection, and magic

Jiutian Xannu (Chinese), the goddess of war, sex, and longevity

Joan of Arc (French Catholic), saint who led battles in Hundred Years War

Judith (Hebrew), warrior and pious widow

Justitia (Roman) or Dike (Greek), the goddess of justice

Kali (Hindu), goddess of time, change, rage, destruction, and resistance

Kuan Jin (Buddhist), goddess of compassion, mercy, and kindness

Lady Fatima (Catholic), saved the life of the pope

Lady Godiva (English), patron saint of churches and seminaries

Lilith (Jewish), early biblical figure (pre-Eve)

Ma'at (Egyptian), goddess of truth, balance, harmony, law, order, and justice

Maîtresse Mambo Erzulie Fréda (aka Mater Dolorosa) (Haitian Vodou), spirit of love, beauty, dance

Malala Yousafzai (Pakistani), activist for female education

Marguerite Porete (French), one of the Beguine (holy women) of the thirteenth century

Marianne Williamson (Spiritualist), self-help author and spiritual leader

Mary Magdalene (Christian), first person to witness the resurrection

Maya (Buddhist), Buddha's mother

Medb (Irish), warrior queen of Connacht

Melpomene (Greek), goddess of tragic performances

Minerva (Roman), goddess of war, or **Athena** (Greek), goddess of handicrafts, professions, arts, and war

Miriam (Jewish), biblical prophetess

Mother Mary (Christian), the mother of Jesus Christ

Mother Nature (common), the personification of the world and all its powers

Mother Teresa (Catholic), Albanian-Indian nun and missionary

Nerrivik (Eskimo), goddess who rules over sea creatures

Niamh (Celtic), queen of the fairies

Ninhursag (Sumerian), goddess of wild and herd animals

Nokomis (Native American), corn mother

Oduduwa (Yoruban), mother goddess and original creator of the earth

Ozwiena (Slavic), goddess of gossip

Pele (Hawaiian), goddess of the volcano

Pema Chödrön (Buddhist), Buddhist nun and writer

Polyhymnia (Greek), goddess personifying hymns

Ruth (Christian/Jewish), great grandmother to the biblical David

Saint Catherine of Siena (Catholic), doctor of the church

Sarah (Christianity), the mother of nations

Sarasvati (Hindu), goddess of knowledge and the arts

Sedna (Inuit), goddess of the sea

Sequana (Gallo-Roman), goddess of ecology

Shekinah (Jewish), mother of fair love, fear, knowledge, and hope

Spider Woman (Navajo), the goddess who taught humans to weave

Saint Adelaide (Catholic), patron saint of abuse victims, parenthood, and family issues

Saint Agrippina (Catholic), patron saint of thunderstorms, leprosy, and evil spirits

Saint Angela Merici (Catholic), patron saint for the sick, disabled, and physically challenged

Saint Quiteria (Catholic), protector against dog bites

Storm (African), fictional superhero

Tara Brach (Buddhist), psychologist, author, meditations

Terpsichore (Greek), goddess representing dance

Thalia (Greek), goddess of comedy

Tiamat (Babylonian), goddess of the monstrous deep

Urama (Greek), goddess of astronomy

Vajrayogini (Tantric/Buddhist), prime deity in Tantra, the essence of all Buddhas

Valkyries (Norse), twelve female figures who decide who lives or dies in battle

Virgin Mary (Christian), mother of Jesus

White Buffalo Calf Woman (Lakota), supernatural woman and prophet

Bibliography

Ackerman, Diane. *The Rarest of the Rare*. New York: Vintage, 1997.

Adams, Cecil. https://www.connectsavannah.com/savannah/did-male-dominance -put-a-stop-to-worshiping-female-goddesses/Content?oid=5003766 21 June 2017 (retrieved November 21, 2020).

Afua, Queen. *Sacred Woman: A Guide to Healing the Feminine Body, Mind, and Spirit*. New York: One World, 2001.

Agha-Jaffar, Tamara. *Women and Goddesses in Myth and Sacred Text: An Anthology*. York: Pearson Education, 2005.

Anand, Anahata. "Divine Balance: The Sacred Union of the Divine Feminine and Masculine." ShamangelicHealing.com, 18 December 2017 (retrieved November 21, 2020).

Anasathwamy, Anil, and Kate Douglas. "The Origins of Sexism. How Men Came to Rule 12,000 Years Ago." *New Scientist*, April, 2018. https://www.newscientist .com/article/mg23831740-400-the-origins-of-sexism-how-men-came-to-rule -12000-years-ago/.

Andrews, Tamra. *Legends of the Earth, Sea, and Sky: An Encyclopedia of Nature Myths*. Oxford: ABC-CLIO, 1998.

Bashford, Sophie. https://www.sophiebashford.com/5-steps-to-awakening-divine -feminine-energy/.

Benowitz, June Melby. *Encyclopedia of American Women and Religion*. Santa Barbara/ Denver/Oxford: ABC-CLIO, 1998.

Besant, Annie. "The Changing World: And Lectures to Theosophical Students." University of California, 1910.

Billington, Sandra, and Miranda Green, Eds. *The Concept of the Goddess*. London and New York: Routledge, 1996.

Bohmbach, Karla. "Daughter of Jephthah: Bible." Jewish Women's Archive. December, 31 1999. https://jwa.org/encyclopedia/article/daughter-of-jephthah-bible.

Bolen, Jean Shinoda. "Discover Your Signature Goddesses (and Gods!) for True Empowerment and Self-Expression." *The Shift Network* (retrieved November 14, 2018).

Book of Judges. Hebrew Bible. https://www.sefaria.org/Judges?lang=bi.

Bowman, Matthew. *The Mormon People: The Making of An American Faith*. New York: Random House, 2012.

Bradford, Hope. *Kuan Yin Buddhism: the Kuan Yin Parables, Visitations, and Teachings*, 2019.

Bhishma, Anushasana Parva. *Mahabharata* 13.47.26.

Britannica.com. "Al-Lat." https://www.britannica.com/topic/al-Lat.

———. "Book of Esther." https://www.britannica.com/topic/Book-of-Esther.

———. "Ishtar." https://www.britannica.com/topic/Ishtar-Mesopotamian-goddess.

Campbell, Joseph, and Charles Muses, eds. *In All Her Names: Explorations of the Feminine in Divinity*. San Francisco: HarperCollins, 1991.

Care.org. "Joint Gender Community Statement on U.S. Foreign Assistance." https://www.care.org/news-and-stories/press-releases/joint-gender-community-statement-on-u-s-foreign-assistance/.

Carson, Rachel. *Silent Spring, The Anniversary Edition*. New York: Houghton-Mifflin, 2002.

Cartwright, Mark. "Amaterasu." Ancient History Encyclopedia, https://www.ancient.eu/Amaterasu/.

Carver, Melissa. "10 Female Archetypes and Leaders to Inspire You." The Chopra Center, October 2016. https://chopra.com/articles/10-female-archetypes-and-leaders-to-inspire-you.

Catholic Online. "St. Adelaide." https://www.catholic.org/saints/saint.php?saint_id=525.

Chang, Pao. "Balancing the Divine Feminine and Divine Masculine Energies." EnergyFanatics.com (retrieved May 14, 2017).

Chodron, Pema. *When Things Fall Apart: Heart Advice for Difficult Times*. Shambahala, 2016.

Christianity Today. "50 Women You Should Know." www.christianitytoday.com/ct/2012/october/50-women-you-should-know.html.

Cleary, Thomas and Sartaz Aziz. *Twilight Goddess: Spiritual Feminism and Feminine Spirituality*. Boston and London: Shambhala, 2000.

Coghlan, Andy. "Ivory 'Venus' is First Depiction of a Woman." https://www.newscientist.com/article/dn17121-ivory-venus-is-first-depiction-of-a-woman/.

Corey, Dan, "A Growing List of Men Accused of Sexual Misconduct since Weinstein." https://www.nbcnews.com/storyline/sexual-misconduct/weinstein-here-s-growing-list-men-accused-sexual-misconduct-n816546.

Coulter, Charles Russell, and Patricia Turner. *Encyclopedia of Ancient Deities*. Jefferson/London: McFarland & Company, Inc., Publishers, 2000.

Crystal, Ellie. "Creation Women." http://www.crystalinks.com/namcreationwomen .html (retrieved November 21, 2020).

Csikszentmihalyi, Mihaly. *Creativity: Flow and the Psychology of Discovery and Invention*. New York: Harper Perennial, 1996.

Daly, Kathleen N. *Greek and Roman Mythology A to Z*. New York: Facts on File, 1992.

Dancing to Eagle Spirit Society. "The Sacred Pipe of White Buffalo Calf Woman." http://www.dancingtoeaglespiritsociety.org/pipe.php (retrieved November 21, 2020).

Das, Rasamandala. *The Illustrated Encyclopedia of Hinduism*. UK: Lorenz Books, 2013.

Daughter RavynStar. "Journeying into the Goddess" blog. journeyingtothegoddess .wordpress.com/author/daughterravynstar/.

Davis, Philip G. *Goddess Unmasked: The Rise of Neopagan Feminist Spirituality*. Dallas: Spence Publishing Company, 1998.

DelMastro, M. *All the Women of the Bible*. Castle Books, 2009.

Dennis, Rabbi Geoffrey W. *The Encyclopedia of Jewish Myth, Magic and Mysticism*. Woodbury, MN: Llewellyn Publications, 2016.

dePizan, Christine. *The Book of the City of Ladies*, 1410.

Ecclesiasticus 24:18-20. The King James Bible online. https://www.kingjamesbible online.org/Ecclesiasticus-24-18/.

Estés, Clarissa Pinkola. *Women Who Run with the Wolves*. New York: Ballantine Books, 1996.

Evans, Rachel Held. *A Year of Biblical Womanhood*. New York: Thomas Nelson, Inc., 2012.

Firestone, Lisa. "Are We Still Condemning Women for their Sexuality?" https:// www.psychalive.org/are-we-still-condemning-women-for-their-sexuality/ (retrieved November 21, 2020).

Flood, Allison. "Publishing industry Is Overwhelmingly White and Female, Us Study Finds." The Guardian.com, 27 Jan 2016. https://www.theguardian.com /books/2016/jan/27/us-study-finds-publishing-is-overwhelmingly-white-and -female.

Ford, Clyde W. *The Hero with the African Face*. New York: Bantam Books, 2000.

Fortune Magazine. "Fortune 500." 2020. https://fortune.com/fortune500/.

Forty, Jo. *Mythology: A Visual Encyclopedia*. New York: PRC Publishing, Inc., 1999.

Fredericks, Bronwyn. "Reempowering Ourselves: Australian Aboriginal Women." *Signs* vol. 35, no. 3. https://www.journals.uchicago.edu/doi/abs/10.1086/648511.

Galland, China. "About China Galland." https://resurrectinglove.org/about/.

———. *Longing for Darkness: Tara and the Black Madonna*. New York: Penguin, 2007.

Garder, Emily. *Women and the Animal Rights Movement*. New York: Rutgers University Press, 2011.

Garling, Wendy. "Three Forgotten Stories about the Buddha's Mother," May 12, 2017, https://tricycle.org/trikedaily/three-forgotten-stories-buddhas-mother/.

Gilbert, Elizabeth. *Big Magic*. New York: Riverhead Books, 2015.

———. "Wisdom & Age & Women." elizabethgilbert.com, 22 June 2014.

Glatz, Carol. "The Number of Priests Declined for First Time in Decade Vatican Says." https://cruxnow.com/vatican/2019/03/number-of-priests-declined-for-first-time-in-decade-vatican-says/.

Godchecker. "Native American Mythology." www.godchecker.com (retrieved November 21, 2020).

———. "Shakaru." http://www.godchecker.com/pantheon/native-american-mythology.php?deity=SHAKARU (retrieved November 21, 2020).

Golden, Carla. "Why and How to Feed the Divine Feminine in Men & Women." CarlaGoldenWellness.com (retrieved December 18, 2019).

The Green Belt Movement. http://www.greenbeltmovement.org/.

Green, Miranda. *Celtic Goddesses: Warriors, Virgins and Mothers*. British Museum Publications, Ltd., 1995.

Guardian, The. "Wonder Woman Announced as UN Ambassador Amid Protest." 2016 October 21. https://www.theguardian.com/books/2016/oct/21/wonder-woman-un-ambassador-staff-protest.

Guerrasio, Jason. "'Wonder Woman' Is Now the Highest-Grossing Superhero Origin Movie of All Time." *Business Insider*. https://www.businessinsider.com/wonder-woman-highest-grossing-superhero-origin-movie-2017-11.

Gyatso, Janet. "Down with the Demoness: Reflections on a Feminine Ground in Tibet." *Feminine Ground: Essays on Women and Tibet*. New York: Snow Lion Publications, 1997.

Hanchin, Vikki. "What Is the Sacred Feminine?" https://www.wisdom2be.com/essays-insights-wisdomwritings-spirituality/what-is-the-sacred-feminine-by-vikki-hanchin-lsw.

Hartmann, Thom. *The Last Hours of Ancient Sunlight.* "Her Story." https://www
.thomhartmann.com/blog/2007/11/last-hours-ancient-sunlight.

Harvey, Andrew and Anne Baring. *The Divine Feminine: Exploring the Feminine
Face of God Around the World.* Berkeley, CA: Conari Press, 1996.

Hehman, Eric, Elana C. Graber, Lindsay H. Hoffman, and Samuel L. Gaertner.
"Warmth and Competence: A Content Analysis of Photographs Depicting American Presidents." https://www.semanticscholar.org/paper/Warmth
-and-Competence%3A-A-Content-Analysis-of-Hehman-Graber
/f8b843d800e2b8013ee28b4c1330e4e3c37a5c42.

Honor the Earth. "Winona LaDuke." https://www.honorearth.org/speaking
_engagements.

International Day of Rural Women. United Nations. October 12, 2018. https://www
.un.org/en/observances/rural-women-day.

"Iroquois Creation Story." http://option.canada.pagesperso-orange.fr/iroquois
_creation.htm.

Jahme, Carole. *Beauty and the Beasts.* New York: Soho Press, 2002.

Johnson, Elizabeth A. *Abounding in Kindness.* New York: Orbis Books, 2015.

Johnson, Megan. "The Healthcare Future Is Female." https://www.athenahealth.com
/knowledge-hub/practice-management/healthcare-future-female, 14 Feb 2018.

Kidd, Sue Monk. *Dance of the Dissident Daughter.* HarperOne, 1996.

Killgrove, Kristina. "Here's How Corsets Deformed the Skeletons of Victorian
Women." *Forbes,* 25 Nov 2015. https://www.forbes.com/sites/kristinakillgrove
/2015/11/16/how-corsets-deformed-the-skeletons-of-victorian-women/?sh
=6ad97c0799cc.

Klassen, Chris, ed. *Feminist Spirituality: The Next Generation.* Lanham, MD: Lexing-
ton Books, 2009.

Knapp, Bettina L. *Women in Myth.* Albany: State University of New York Press,
1997.

———. *Women, Myth, and the Feminine Principle.* Albany: State University of New
York Press, 1998.

Kraemer, Ross Sheppard. *Her Share of the Blessings: Women's Religions Among
Pagans, Jews, and Christians in the Greco-Roman World.* New York: Oxford University Press, 1994.

Kristoff, Nicholas, and Sheryl WuDunn. *Half the Sky: Turning Oppression into
Opportunity for Women.* New York: Knopf, 2008.

LaDuke, Winona. www.honorearth.org (retrieved November 21, 2020).

Lamott, Anne. *Plan B: Further Thoughts on Faith*. New York: Riverhead Books, 2005.

LaPlant, Robbyne. "2017—The Year of the Goddess Awakening and the Divine Feminine Returning." https://www.whitewolfjourneys.com/special-messages/2017-year-goddess-awakening-divine-feminine-returning/ (retrieved December 3, 2019).

Larrington, Carolyne. *The Norse Myths: A Guide to the Gods and Heroes*. New York: Thames and Hudson, 2017.

Lee and Low. The Diversity Baseline Survey. https://www.leeandlow.com/about-us/the-diversity-baseline-survey.

Leeming, David. *Creation Myths of the World Encyclopedia*. New York: ABC-CLIO, 2010.

Leeming, David, and Jake Page. *Myths of the Female Divine Goddess*. New York: Oxford University Press, 1994.

Lemut, Nika. *Ozwiena's Echo*. https://ryuutsu.artstation.com/projects/XrBVa.

Lim, Clarissa-Jan. "Societies Where Women Rule (Literally) Do Exist—Here's How They're Different From Ours." https://aplus.com/a/matriarchal-societies-different-mainstream?no_monetization=true (retrieved November 21, 2020).

Lindeman, Lenore. "The Legend of Senda the Sea Goddess." www.polarlife.ca/Traditional/myth/sedna.htm.

Lipka, Michael. "U.S. Nuns Face Shrinking Numbers and Tensions with the Vatican." Pew Research Center. https://www.pewresearch.org/fact-tank/2014/08/08/u-s-nuns-face-shrinking-numbers-and-tensions-with-the-vatican/.

Madsen, Pamela. "The Divine Feminine? The Awakened Masculine? Huh?" https://www.psychologytoday.com/us/blog/shameless-woman/201103/the-divine-feminine-the-awakened-masculine-huh (retrieved November 21, 2020).

Malala.org. The official website of Malala Yousafzi. November 21, 2020.

Mark, Joshua L. "Female Physicians in Ancient Egypt." World History Encyclopedia, https://www.worldhistory.org/article/49/female-physicians-in-ancient-egypt/.

Mastro, M.L. del. *All the Women of the Bible*. New York: Castle Books, 2006.

Matthews, Caitlin. *Sophia Goddess of Wisdom: The Divine Feminine from Black Goddess to World-Soul*. London: Thorsons, 1992.

Mellor, Mary. *Feminism & Ecology*. New York: New York University Press, 1997.

Melton, J. Gordon and Martin Baumann, eds. *Religions of the World Volumes 1–4*. Santa Barbara/Denver/Oxford: ABC-CLIO, 2002.

Mercier, Maureen. "Sacred Feminine: Qualities of the Divine Feminine Goddess." http://pyschicreiki.com/sacred-feminine.html (retrieved October 30, 2020).

Merriam-Webster. "Man-made." 2021. https://www.merriam-webster.com /dictionary/man-made.

McDermott, Rose. *Political Psychology in International Relations*, University of Michigan Press, 2004.

Monaghan, Patricia. *Encyclopedia of Goddesses & Heroines*. Novato, CA: New World Library, 2014.

Mother-God.com. "Divine Mother, Ma-Tsu." http://www.mother-god.com/ma-tsu .html.

Mulheres da Terra. http://mulheresdaterra.com.br/wp_en/ (retrieved November 1, 2020).

Nivedita, Sister. *The Complete Works of Sister Nivedita*. Advaita Ashrama, 2012.

Noda, Moeko. "Authors in Conversation: Interview with Elizabeth Gilbert, Part One." KonMari Media, 2018. https://konmari.com/marie-kondo -interviews-elizabeth-gilbert/.

"Ntozake Shange." *Poets*. Accessed October 29, 2020. https://poets.org/poet /ntozake-shange#poet__works.

Nyborg, Marilyn. "Turning the World Right Side Up: The Feminine Remedy." https://www.wisdom2be.com/essays-insights-wisdomwritings-spirituality /turning-the-world-right-side-up-the-feminine-remedy-by-marilyn-nyborg.

OldWolf, Brian. "The Complete Guide. The Nine Muses of Greek Mythology." https://owlcation.com/humanities/The-Muses-The-Nine-Muses-Goddesses -of-Greek-Mythology.

Oleary, Hernanday. "When and why did Egyptians stop worshipping their ancient gods?" https://www.quora.com/When-and-why-did-the-Egyptians-stop -worshipping-their-ancient-gods (retrieved November 21, 2020).

ORACC Museum. "Tiamat (goddess)." http://oracc.museum.upenn.edu/amgg /listofdeities/tiamat/index.html (retrieved November 19, 2020).

Orangutan.org. "Biography, Dr. Birute Mary Galdikas." https://orangutan.org/about /dr-birute-mary-galdikas/.

Oxford Reference. "Odudwa, Locked in the Darkness, in a Calabash." https://www .oxfordreference.com/view/10.1093/oi/authority.20110803100245987.

Parker, Lauren. "The Future Isn't Female, It's Trans." www.laurenparker.com (retrieved September 5, 2020).

Paul, Diana Y. *Women in Buddhism: Images of the Feminine in the Mahayana Tradition*. Berkeley/Los Angeles/London: University of California Press, 1979.

"Pawnee Creation Myth." http://www.bigorrin.org/archive119.htm.

PBS.org. "Thunder, Perfect Mind." Interview with Elaine Pagels. https://www.pbs.org/wgbh/pages/frontline/shows/religion/maps/primary/thunder.html.

Pew Research Center. "The Gender Gap in Religion Around the World." https://www.pewforum.org/2016/03/22/the-gender-gap-in-religion-around-the-world/.

———. "U.S. Nuns Face Shrinking Numbers and Tensions with the Vatican." https://www.pewresearch.org/fact-tank/2014/08/08/u-s-nuns-face-shrinking-numbers-and-tensions-with-the-vatican/.

Purdue University. "Modules on Jacques Lacan." https://cla.purdue.edu/academic/english/theory/psychoanalysis/lacandevelop.html.

Quarrie, Deanne. "Sequana and Blessed Water." Feminism and Religion.com. (retrieved January 15, 2020).

Rajhans, Shri Gyan. "The Goddess Durga: The Mother of the Hindu Universe." https://www.thoughtco.com/goddess-durga-1770363 November 21, 2020.

Ramesh. "1000 Names of Goddess Durga-Devi Parvati," Detechter.com. https://detechter.com/1000-names-goddess-durga-devi-parvati/.

Raudvere, Catharina. *More than Mythology*. Nordic Academic Press, 2012.

RC, Dola. "The Obscure World of Early Women Artists in Japan." https://angiesdiary.com/lifestyle/the-obscure-world-of-early-women-artists-of-japan/ (retrieved November 1, 2020).

Redmond, Layne. *When Drummers Were Women: A Spiritual History of Women*. Three Rivers Press, 1997.

Resonant Mind. "Tao Te Ching, Verse 6." https://www.resonantmind.org/tao-te-ching-verse-6-explained/.

Riggio, Ronald E. "Women's Intuition: Myth or Reality?" *Psychology Today* (retrieved November 21, 2020). https://www.psychologytoday.com/za/blog/cutting-edge-leadership/201107/women-s-intuition-myth-or-reality.

Rodriguez, Santiago. Latinx Theology books. https://Sojo.net/articles/latinx-theology-reading-list (retrieved August 15, 2020).

Rothenberg, Albert, M.D. *Creativity & Madness: New Findings and Old Stereotypes*. Baltimore/London: Johns Hopkins University Press, 1990.

Rumi, Robin. "Writing about Spirituality, Love and Connection." Robinrumi.com.

Saari, Peggy and Elizabeth Shaw. *Witchcraft in America*. Detroit/San Francisco /London/Boston Woodbridge: UXL, 2001.

Sacred-texts.com. "Eskimo Folk Tales." http://www.sacred-texts.com/nam/inu/eft /eft43.htm (retrieved November 21, 2020).

Sandstrom, Aleksandra. "Women Relatively Rare in Top Positions of Religious Leadership." https://www.pewresearch.org/fact-tank/2016/03/02 /women-relatively-rare-in-top-positions-of-religious-leadership/.

Sarton, May. *Journal of a Solitude*. New York: WW Norton, 1992.

Scholes, Lucy. "The Female-Only Book Club." TLS online, April 20, 2020. https:// www.the-tls.co.uk/articles/why-women-read-more-fiction-helen-taylor-review -lucy-scholes/.

Sebastian, Joseph. *God as Feminine: A Dialogue*. Frankfurt, Germany: Peter Lang, 1995.

Shange, Ntozake. *For Colored Girls Who Have Considered Suicide/When the Rainbow Is Enuf,* New York: Scribner, 1999.

Shendruk, Amanda. "Analyzing the Gender Representation of 34,476 Comic Book Characters." Pudding. https://pudding.cool/2017/07/comics.

Shikoba. Wild Women Sisterhood. www.wildwomensisterhood.com.

Smithsonian Art Museum. "Edmonia Lewis." https://americanart.si.edu/artist /edmonia-lewis-2914 (retrieved November 21, 2020).

Specia, Megan. "Saudi Arabia Granted Women the Right to Drive. A Year On, It's Still Complicated." *New York Times*, 24 June 2019.

Spencer, Charles. Full text of Oration at Princess Diana's funeral. http://www.bbc .co.uk/news/special/politics97/diana/spencerfull.html.

Starhawk, Diane Baker, and Anne Hill. *Circle Round: Raising Children in Goddess Traditions*. New York: Bantam Books, 2000.

Stewart, Emily. "Women Are Running for Office in Record Numbers. In Corporate America, They're Losing Ground." Vox.com. March 15, 2020.

Stone, Merlin. *Ancient Mirrors of Womanhood: Our Goddess and Heroine Heritage*. New York: New Sibylline Books, 1979.

Teish, Luisah. *On Holy Ground: Commitment and Devotion to Sacred Lands*. Daughters of the Goddess, 2013.

Tharp, Twyla. *The Creative Habit: Learn It and Use It for Life*. New York: Simon & Schuster, 2003.

Timelessmyths.com. "Gaea." https://www.timelessmyths.com/classical/primeval
.html#Gaea.

Toomey, Christine. *In Search of Buddha's Daughters.* New York: The Experiment, 2015.

toppr.com. "The Start of Farming and Herding." Retrieved November 21, 2020.
https://www.toppr.com/guides/history/from-gathering-to-growing-food
/the-start-of-farming-and-herding/.

Treesisters. "Berta Isabel Cáceres Flores." https://treesisters.org/blog/the-life
-of-berta-caceres.

UN Commission on the Status of Women. "UN Women statement on the International Day of Rural Women." October 11, 2018. https://www.un.org/en
/observances/rural-women-day.

Vaughan-Lee, Llewellyn. "Reclaiming the Feminine Mystery of Creation." When-
TheSoulAwakens.org, 2007 (retrieved January 20, 2020).

Vivekananda, Swami. *The Complete Works of Swami Vivekananda/Volume 9/
Excerpts from Sister Nivedita's Book/VIII The Temple Of Pandrenthan.* https://
en.wikisource.org/wiki/The_Complete_Works_of_Swami_Vivekananda/Volume
_9/Excerpts_from_Sister_Nivedita%27s_Book/VIII_The_Temple_Of_Pandrenthan.

Waldherr, Kris. *Doomed Queens: Royal Women Who Met Bad Ends, From Cleopatra
to Princess Di.* Crown: 2008.

Wells, Rebecca. *Divine Secrets of the Ya-Ya Sisterhood.* HarperCollins, 1996.

Wensley, Kelly. "The Four Life Phases of a Woman." ElephantJournal.com, 2013.

Whitmont, Edward C. *Return of the Goddess.* New York: Crossroad, 1982.

Williams, Hattie. "More Women Than Men Enter Clergy Training, Latest Figures
Show." ChurchTimesUK, 25 September 2017.

Willis, Janice D. "Tibetan An-s: The Nun's Life in Tibet." *Feminine Ground: Essays on
Women and Tibet.* New York: Snow Lion Publications, 1997.

Wiseman, Sara. SaraWiseman.com.

Wollstonecraft, Mary. "A Vindication of the Rights of Women." 1792. https://www
.unlv.edu/sites/default/files/page_files/1635/Mar.4-Wollstonecraft-reading.pdf.

Women and Life on Earth. www.wloe.org.

Wood, Juliette, *Concept of the Goddess.* New York: Routledge, 1997.

Wrenn, Corey. Vegan Feminist Network. http://veganfeministnetwork.com/.

Younis, Omar. "California's 'Weed Nuns' on a Mission to Heal with Cannabis." Reu-
ters.com (retrieved November 1, 2020).